Causation: A Very Short Introduction

VERY SHORT INTRODUCTIONS are for anyone wanting a stimulating and accessible way in to a new subject. They are written by experts, and have been translated into more than 40 different languages.

The Series began in 1995, and now covers a wide variety of topics in every discipline. The VSI library now contains over 350 volumes—a Very Short Introduction to everything from Psychology and Philosophy of Science to American History and Relativity—and continues to grow in every subject area.

Very Short Introductions available now

ADVERTISING Winston Fletcher
AFRICAN HISTORY John Parker and
    Richard Rathbone
AGNOSTICISM Robin Le Poidevin
AMERICAN HISTORY Paul S. Boyer
AMERICAN IMMIGRATION
    David A. Gerber
AMERICAN POLITICAL PARTIES
    AND ELECTIONS L. Sandy Maisel
AMERICAN POLITICS
    Richard M. Valelly
THE AMERICAN PRESIDENCY
    Charles O. Jones
ANAESTHESIA Aidan O'Donnell
ANARCHISM Colin Ward
ANCIENT EGYPT Ian Shaw
ANCIENT GREECE Paul Cartledge
ANCIENT PHILOSOPHY Julia Annas
ANCIENT WARFARE
    Harry Sidebottom
ANGELS David Albert Jones
ANGLICANISM Mark Chapman
THE ANGLO-SAXON AGE John Blair
THE ANIMAL KINGDOM
    Peter Holland
ANIMAL RIGHTS David DeGrazia
THE ANTARCTIC Klaus Dodds
ANTISEMITISM Steven Beller
ANXIETY Daniel Freeman and
    Jason Freeman
THE APOCRYPHAL GOSPELS
    Paul Foster
ARCHAEOLOGY Paul Bahn
ARCHITECTURE Andrew Ballantyne

ARISTOCRACY William Doyle
ARISTOTLE Jonathan Barnes
ART HISTORY Dana Arnold
ART THEORY Cynthia Freeland
ASTROBIOLOGY David C. Catling
ATHEISM Julian Baggini
AUGUSTINE Henry Chadwick
AUSTRALIA Kenneth Morgan
AUTISM Uta Frith
THE AVANT GARDE David Cottington
THE AZTECS David Carrasco
BACTERIA Sebastian G. B. Amyes
BARTHES Jonathan Culler
THE BEATS David Sterritt
BEAUTY Roger Scruton
BESTSELLERS John Sutherland
THE BIBLE John Riches
BIBLICAL ARCHAEOLOGY
    Eric H. Cline
BIOGRAPHY Hermione Lee
THE BLUES Elijah Wald
THE BOOK OF MORMON
    Terryl Givens
BORDERS Alexander C. Diener and
    Joshua Hagen
THE BRAIN Michael O'Shea
THE BRITISH CONSTITUTION
    Martin Loughlin
THE BRITISH EMPIRE Ashley Jackson
BRITISH POLITICS Anthony Wright
BUDDHA Michael Carrithers
BUDDHISM Damien Keown
BUDDHIST ETHICS Damien Keown
CANCER Nicholas James

For more information visit our website

www.oup.com/vsi/

Stephen Mumford and Rani Lill Anjum

CAUSATION

A Very Short Introduction

OXFORD
UNIVERSITY PRESS

OXFORD
UNIVERSITY PRESS

Great Clarendon Street, Oxford, ox2 6DP,
United Kingdom

Oxford University Press is a department of the University of Oxford.
It furthers the University's objective of excellence in research, scholarship,
and education by publishing worldwide. Oxford is a registered trade mark of
Oxford University Press in the UK and in certain other countries

© Stephen Mumford and Rani Lill Anjum 2013

The moral rights of the authors have been asserted

First Edition published in 2013

Impression: 9

Published in the United States of America by Oxford University Press
198 Madison Avenue, New York, NY 10016, United States of America

British Library Cataloguing in Publication Data
Data available

Library of Congress Control Number: 2013941081

ISBN 978-0-19-968443-4

Printed and bound by
CPI Group (UK) Ltd, Croydon, CRO 4YY

Contents

List of illustrations

The publisher and the author apologize for any errors or omissions
in the above list. If contacted they will be happy to rectify these at the
earliest opportunity.

Why causation?

Causation is the most fundamental connection in the universe. Without it, there is no moral responsibility: none of our thoughts would be connected with our actions and none of our actions with any consequences. Nor would we have a system of law because blame resides only in someone having caused injury or damage. There would be no science or technology. Any intervention we make in the world around us is premised on there being causal connections that are to at least a degree predictable. It is causation that is the basis of this prediction and also of explanation.

But what is it for one thing to cause another, such as when a stone smashes a window or an oil slick causes a skid and a crash? Philosophers have struggled with this question for millennia, at least since Aristotle (384–322 BC). They approach the problem in the abstract while scientists encounter it in its concrete instances. The sciences are full of causal claims and a scientist is bound to wonder at some point what it is they are dealing with exactly.

There are a number of views. Some think the basis of causation is regularity: that one thing or event is constantly conjoined with another. Others have said that this is neither sufficient nor necessary for a causal connection. Another theory is that the existence of the effect depends on the existence of the cause; but does this adequately distinguish causes from other, related

phenomena? This *Very Short Introduction* will introduce the
reader to the key theories of causation and also the surrounding
debates and controversies. Do causes produce their effects by
guaranteeing them? Do causes have to precede their effects? Can
causation be reduced to the forces of physics? And are we right to
think of causation as one single thing at all?

We will not shy away from the disputed territory of causation.
Rather, we will be open about the fact that there is yet to be a final
consensus on this most immediate and vital element of the world.
Without attempting a systematic survey, we will introduce the
reader to what is one of the core topics in philosophy. But the book
is not only for philosophers. Every engineer and pharmacist is
working with causation; indeed, none of us has any other choice.
Without it, none of our interventions in the world would have any
point. And in other sciences the most common form of
explanation is a causal explanation, and prediction is premised on
the known causal laws. Causation is just as much an integral part
of physics, biology, chemistry, geology, meteorology, astronomy,
and oceanography as it is of philosophy. And we should not forget
the social sciences—economics, history, sociology, anthropology,
psychology, education, political science, and law—where causal
claims are equally ubiquitous.

Like a number of other areas of philosophy, causation is a topic
that could intimidate the novice because of its abstract and
technical nature. Many of the basic ideas, concepts, and questions
of causation are simple enough, however, and we aim to explain
and motivate the key issues without the aid of technical
vocabulary.

Only if we are armed with a theory of causation will we be able to go
out and look for it. Improving one's theory of causation—through
philosophy—should thus improve the process of discovering causes.
This can be a vital task. Lives depend on identifying the causes of
certain diseases and, of course, on finding medicines that can cause

recovery from them. And we can only hope to bring climate change under control once we have understood what causes it. The causes of war, poverty, suffering, and pain are all things that we need to identify and avoid. In their place, we should promote the causes of stability, peace, and prosperity. But how could we even hope to find these things if we do not understand what it is for one thing to cause another? Here is the place to start for anyone who needs to know this, which we argue is everyone.

Chapter 1

The problem: what's the matter with causation?

An invasion of rats sweeps through town. They fill the streets, eating from rubbish bins and invading homes. The townsfolk have never seen the like before and their attempt to repel and exterminate the rodent visitors is a losing battle. A few days after the rats first arrive, people start getting ill with an unpleasant stomach bug, some cases of which are life threatening. The disease spreads, affecting the majority of the town's population. Neither the rat invasion nor the epidemic had occurred there before. Someone raises the inevitable question: Did the rats cause the disease?

Perhaps it looks like an open-and-shut case against the rats. A new factor was introduced into the local environment and was quickly followed by a spread of illness. But did one thing cause the other? Perhaps it was mere coincidence that people got ill just after the rats arrived. Or there might have been a different factor that brought the disease: one young lady had just returned from an exotic holiday looking none too good. Perhaps she brought the bug.

The problem shows the importance of identifying causes. If the rats are responsible for the continued spread of disease, then their containment or eradication will probably be a high priority. But if the causes lie elsewhere, the rat problem can wait.

There is nevertheless a prior question. How can we even start looking for the causes, of a disease or whatever, before we have some understanding of what it is for one thing to be a cause of another? Surely we have to know what causation is before we start saying that this was the cause of that. We need a theory of causation. And anyone who makes a causal claim must have such a theory, whatever it may be, otherwise the claim would be empty.

One such theory—not a very sophisticated one—could be based on the fact that there was no disease in town before the rats came, therefore the rats caused it. The theory coming out of that observation might be formulated as follows: a cause is a new factor that has been introduced and that precedes a conspicuous change. But we will see that we should be able to do better than that. Causation is likely to be more complex than such a basic definition would allow. The task ahead of us is to explain some of the complexities involved.

Being philosophical

The question we are asking is a specifically philosophical one. What is causation? It is initially a conceptual question: What do we *mean* by causation? But it could easily advance from that to a question of what is the real-world essence of causation, which is more of an ontological one: What *is* causation? But we needn't get too far into the distinction between conceptual and ontological at this stage. The point is that these questions are not ones that we can settle simply by recourse to experience.

Science deals with matters that should ultimately be settled by the evidence of the senses. Often there is an interplay between theory and observation and many theories are thought viable long before they can be tested empirically. Empirical evidence is the evidence we gain through our observations, whether unaided or with the use of devices such as microscopes and oscilloscopes. Empirical testing remains the mark of science and is thought the ultimate tribunal of scientific truth.

And on the issue of what causes what, we should of course grant this to be an empirical matter. We can let the scientists decide what causes solar flares, drought, chemical bonding, cancer, and Down's syndrome. Social scientists can tell us what causes inflation or social unrest. And we can judge on more mundane and domestic causal matters ourselves from the empirical evidence we have available, for instance that the dog always barks when the post arrives.

The methods of philosophy are slightly different. It is not the easiest task to state exactly what they are as the nature of philosophy is itself one of the topics of philosophical debate. Traditionally, however, it is understood to be non-empirical in that philosophical truths are not settled primarily through recourse to experience. Consider a philosophical theory in ethics, for example, that the good is that which procures the greatest happiness of the greatest number. This ethical theory is called utilitarianism. The point is that the evidence of our senses doesn't seem to help us decide whether this theory—of what the good consists in—is right or not.

How do we decide on such questions? A traditional answer is that we use our reason to explore and settle philosophical questions. We consider likely theories and test them against hypothetical scenarios to see if they remain intuitively appealing. Some experience of the world is of course needed in order to acquire our basic concepts and be able to talk about anything at all. But once this has been acquired, it seems that we are able to reason about it in fairly abstract terms. Using just our thinking, we might decide that knowledge consists in justified, true belief or that an equal distribution of wealth would be morally more defensible than an unequal one.

This is the kind of approach that will be taken in this book. We will try to use our thinking to reason through such questions as whether causes must always occur before their effects. Is there any absurdity in supposing so; or any in supposing not so? And what then would be at the core of a credible account of causation? We will also be assuming the priority of philosophy in these matters, by which we mean that the basic philosophical commitments must come first, before the empirical investigation into their application. In simple terms, this means that we have to know what causation is before we can start to look for it. At least we must have some idea of it.

Let us consider another causal scenario by way of illustration. Suppose we trial a drug on a group of patients and 50 per cent subsequently die. Such an outcome sounds alarming and one might conclude that the drug is harmful. Can we say straight away that this drug kills half of those who take it?

The first thing to point out about the example is that it shows how widespread causal claims are. If you say that this drug—or anything else, for that matter—kills, you are making a causal claim. You are effectively saying that it causes death. Similarly, if a rock breaks a window, Jane upsets John, a noise wakes the baby, or a machine drills a hole, then causal claims are being made. To break, upset, wake, and drill are all causal verbs that we use to make specific claims about causation. All of them seem to involve one thing making another happen. It is what exactly this consists in that is our topic. And we can see, therefore, that while it is a philosophical issue, it is one in which all empirical disciplines have an interest because they are often full of causal claims.

Second, we can question the plausibility of any causal claim in the drug case, based on just this information. Simply that a patient died after taking the drug is no sure sign that the drug was the cause of death. What if all those who took the drug also had an illness of which the expected death rate within that same time

1. David Hume, who couldn't see causation

span was 80 per cent? That information puts the issue in a
different light. Although many who took the drug died, it might be
that the drug was not harmful at all. Perhaps it prevented a
number of deaths or increased the length of life of those suffering
the illness. And even if this is not the scenario, there might be an
even simpler explanation of the deaths. Perhaps after taking the
drug, there was a cataclysmic earthquake that affected the area in
which it was trialled. There could be a far more plausible
explanation of the deaths than the action of the drug.

What philosophical conclusions might one then draw? The immediate lesson seems to be that causation requires more than one thing being followed by another. A man might take a pill and then die, or touch a rat and then die, but for us to say that the pill or the rat caused the man's death, we need something more. It is this something more—the causal connection—that we will be investigating in the rest of the book.

The elusive cause

An important point lurks in the background of this discussion and we should now articulate it. David Hume (1711–76) promoted an idea, which continues to attract adherents, that there is something elusive about causation that makes it a particularly difficult matter to know. This is a claim that could be challenged but first we should try to understand it.

In his 1739 book *A Treatise of Human Nature* (Book I, Part III, Section VI) Hume argued that all we can observe in nature is a series of events. One thing happens and then another, and then another, and so on. The problem when we start wondering about whether any of those events are causally connected is that the supposed causal connection is not itself part of our experience. A match is struck, for instance, and then almost immediately that same match lights. But what we cannot see is that the striking of the match caused it to light, at least according to Hume's account.

How much simpler would it be to make causal claims if it was just a matter of seeing the causal connection tying the two events together, like a rope? Instead, all we see are the two events, the striking of the match and its lighting. The causal connection itself seems unobservable. It hides away and we have to infer its presence from other factors of the situation.

This is why we often struggle to pin down causal connections. To a large extent it is a vast scientific endeavour to figure out what causes what and even when we think causation has been established there is no guarantee that we are right. In the case of the rats, for instance, it was a matter of looking to the wider context of the situation to see if something else could have caused the epidemic. There is always the possibility that the real cause has not yet been discovered.

Bertrand Russell flexes his muscle

Because causation doesn't exactly hit you in the face, there are even some who deny that it exists at all. There are weaker and stronger ways of stating this view. The weaker would be a reductive strategy, which would be to claim that what we commonly take to be causation is actually just something else: something far less mysterious and elusive. This is to make a move that is familiar in philosophy: to explain a problematic phenomenon in other terms that are arguably less so. The reductionist is not denying that there is causation, but they are denying that it is an additional thing in the world, over and above other, more familiar elements. We will be looking at a number of reductive accounts in the chapters that follow.

The stronger kind of strategy, however, could be called eliminativist. The idea here is to find some reason to eliminate a certain category of thing from our considerations altogether. The claim applied to the current topic would be that causation does not exist at all. Whereas the reductionist says that what we took to be causation was actually something else—something that is more obviously part of the world—the eliminativist says simply that there is no causation. Nothing in reality matches that for which we thought we needed the notion of cause.

As an example of such eliminativism we might take Bertrand Russell's classic 1913 paper 'On the Notion of Cause'. Russell (1872–1970) pointed out that although we conceptualize the world in causal terms, if we instead defer to the way physics understands things, we will see that causation has no place.

The notions of causation that philosophers have produced involve asymmetry, Russell noted. The cause produces the effect, for example, and does so asymmetrically. This means that the effect cannot then produce the cause. Causation has a direction. Hence, if the throwing of a stone caused a window to break, then the breaking of the window did not cause the stone to be thrown. That seems to make perfectly good sense to us but Russell thought that common sense, and even philosophy, should be prepared to defer to the expertise of science, and physics in particular.

Russell noted that in science, asymmetric causal relations don't appear at all. Rather, physics is full of equations such as $E = mc^2$ and $F = Gm_1m_2/d^2$. And an equation can be read left to right or right to left. In other words, the directionality of causation is not really a feature of the world because in its scientific formulation it can just as easily run in the opposite direction. There is thus no reason in principle why the breaking of a window couldn't cause a rock to be thrown at it. This would be unproblematic from a mathematical point of view in physics. The causal conceptualization of the world is thus an ignorant and prescientific one and, in a famous passage, Russell says: 'The law of causality, I believe, like much that passes muster among philosophers, is a relic of a bygone age, surviving, like the monarchy, only because it is erroneously supposed to do no harm.'

Russell's view still has some adherents in philosophy but why has it not prevailed? We still do use causal concepts all the time and physics itself has not seen a wholesale abandonment of asymmetric relations. In the first place, we can note that the reading of the equals sign ' = ' is not unambiguous. We become used to it in arithmetic where it indicates an equivalence but it is one that seems to permit at least some directionality. We say that $2 + 2 = 4$, for instance, which is to say that each side is of equal sum. But it is less obvious that $4 = 2 + 2$ insofar as 4 can also be the sum of $1 + 3$. The point is that $2 + 2$ can equal only one sum, 4; whereas 4 can be the sum of several combinations (2 and 2, 1 and

3, 10 and minus 6, and so on). And in this respect there is at least some asymmetry.

This consideration can be brought to bear on the equations of physics because they also are indicative of equivalent magnitudes. From a specific value of m and c, one can derive only one value for E in $E = mc^2$. But for any value of E, there is an infinite number of values for m and c that would produce an equivalence. And there is thus still some asymmetry that needs to be explained. It is not clear, therefore, that an equation automatically rules out asymmetry.

Second, Russell's account was based on his understanding of the physics of 1913. There have been a number of attempts by physicists to put asymmetry back into physical theory. One such notion is entropy, which is an irreversible thermodynamic property. Physics is still a developing science, even though its successes allow us to do so much. We cannot take the case against causation to be settled, in the way Russell thought, because the final physical theory of everything is not yet with us and may never be.

Metaphysics and better physics

This brings us to a third, and perhaps the biggest, consideration against Russell's view. Physics provides a representation of the world: a largely mathematical one. It is useful that it does so. Results within a mathematical model are sometimes borne out and used in explanation, prediction, and technology. But we should not forget that physics is the representation and should not be mistaken for the world itself.

In that case, if we felt that physics had left out of its representation a central datum about the world—the asymmetry of causation—then we might be entitled to ask for a better physics. The world is not a number, nor an equation. It is a concrete particular inhabited by physical objects and some of them appear to be causally related to others. Physics sometimes forces us to rethink and revise common sense, which may be perfectly legitimate. But it should not follow automatically that because a theory works out mathematically, within a model, the world is exactly like that model or like the maths. That is still open for debate. A belief in causation may well be a philosophical one—a metaphysical one, even—but there may be occasions where we can ask for a better physics: one that reflects our metaphysical commitments.

And here, we would maintain, there is much debate still to be had. Willard Van Orman Quine (1908–2000) talked about our beliefs forming an interconnected web. All were open to revision in the light of new evidence but some of them were more central within the web. We would not easily give up our belief in logic, for instance, because it is central to everything else that we believe. We would always try to sacrifice a more peripheral belief first, if it clashed.

A belief in causation, we would maintain, is a very central one. Causation matters so much. Nothing that occurs would have any real significance unless it was causally connected with other things. One might not even mind being beheaded but for the fact that it is a cause of death, pain, inconvenience, and whatever. That lawyers sue for damages is premised on harm being caused. That medicines are worth discovering is premised on them being potential causes of health. And that the Earth revolves around the Sun is determined by it having a gravitational effect on us. Without causation, nothing in our universe would seem to hang together. Hume even called it 'the cement of the universe' ('Abstract of the *Treatise*', 1740).

Now if we were to jettison causation from our web of belief, so much else would have to go with it. It would require an entire reconceptualization of the world and almost everything we have ever believed about it. That is not to say that it is impossible or inconceivable, but that the evidence requiring it had better be very, very good. As we have seen, the theories of physics remain tentative and open to interpretation. In that case, we would argue that we have not yet reached the point Russell thought we had, where we ought to abolish causation.

We will therefore proceed on the basis that causation is a real feature of the world. Indeed, we stand by the argument that it is a vital and central component, without which things would look so different. There would be no cement of the universe. When you strike a match, you expect that it will light. Sometimes that expectation is disappointed but the world is predictable to at least some degree. If the wind blows, the match might not light but at least we know that the match cannot evaporate or transform into a frog. The relative order and predictability of the world seem founded on its causal connections. Having claimed it as a legitimate object of study, we will now proceed to look at some of causation's alleged features. Along the way, some of the leading theories will emerge.

Chapter 2
Regularity: causation without connection?

The world contains many regularities. A regularity is where one kind of thing is associated with or followed by another kind of thing. Water being heated is regularly followed by its turning to steam, for instance. There is no shortage of such examples. Ice being heated is followed by its melting, people eating vegetables is followed by their being healthy, people not eating food is followed by their growing thin and ill, rocks being thrown at windows is followed by those windows breaking, the clapping of hands comes along with a certain kind of sound, unsuspended objects fall to the ground, and so on. We can see the diversity of such cases but they all have something in common. Types of events, actions or states seem to come in pairs where if we have the first, such as a handclap, we have the second, a distinctive kind of sound.

Why do we have these regular associations of types of event? Why do they pair up? There is a very obvious and natural answer: it is because the first type of event is a cause of the second. The heating of ice causes it to melt, for instance, so it is no accident that melting follows the heating. The heating made the melting happen. But do we have good grounds to say this? Does causation explain regularity?

Hume gave us a totally new way of looking at causation and many have found his ideas compelling. His innovation was to turn the problem of causation and correlation on its head. Hume thought that we couldn't say that causation explains correlation. On the contrary, correlation explains causation. We shouldn't say that one kind of thing regularly follows another because they are causally connected. Rather, we think that one thing causes another only because one regularly follows another.

Playing billiards with Hume

How could Hume go against common sense in this way? What was he thinking? He was one of the great empiricist philosophers and the empiricists thought it important to go back to the evidence of the senses. In particular, Hume thought that to understand what our ideas and concepts were about we should consult the original experiences from which they were derived. But if we cast aside the presuppositions of common sense, our experience shows us only that one thing follows another; never that one thing is connected with another, compels it, produces it, or makes it happen.

The 'perfect instance' of causation, Hume said, could be found on the billiard table. One ball moves towards another, they touch, and the second ball, which had previously been stationary, then moves away. We are pretty certain that the first ball, through its contact, caused the second to move. But why do we believe this? What evidence do we have from our senses? What does the belief consist in?

Hume argues that all we see are events following in succession. When you see a player make a shot, you see on the table events occurring in a particular order: let us just call them a, b, c, d, etc. The cue is drawn back, thrusts forward, it touches the white cue ball, the cue ball rolls along the table, it touches a red object ball, there is a sound when the balls touch, the red ball moves away, the cue ball changes direction and slows down. We could go on.

Often causal language is used when describing such sequences. One might say that when the balls touch they 'make' a sound. This suggests that the sound is produced by the balls touching. But as the case is described so far, all we know from experience is the sequence of events. We have no direct experiential evidence that connects the touching of the balls with the sound.

Why, then, should we think that one kind of event caused another if all we know is a sequence of events? Hume has an answer. We could not know that one thing caused another just from observing a single instance, such as just one ball touching another and the second moving away. But in our experience we have no doubt seen many more than just one such instance. We have seen many games of billiards and snooker, where each such game has involved many shots and many such collisions of cue ball and object ball. And what we have known is that in each such case, when one ball hit another, the second started to move having previously been stationary.

Hume's theory was that it is only through observation of regularities that we get any idea at all of causation. Repetition is the key. One type of event is always followed by another and this is what leads us to believe that the first type of event caused the second

Hume's mosaic

There is nothing in Hume's account that allows for an idea of causal production, except insofar as Hume thinks that all we could mean by production is that there is a regular succession of one type of thing followed by another. We saw how the problem of causation is that there is no observable connection that ties the cause to the effect. On Hume's empiricist view, therefore, we have no reason to even believe in a causal connection, since there is no sense impression of it. We thus have a notion of cause that contains no real connection. This Hume acknowledges explicitly, saying: 'All events seem entirely loose and separate. One event follows another; but we never can observe any tie between them. They seem *conjoined*, but never *connected* (*An Enquiry Concerning Human Understanding*, section VII, part 2).

A latter-day Humean, David Lewis (1941–2001), suggested we understand Hume's idea as follows. The world is like a vast mosaic of unconnected matters of fact: just one little thing and then another. But when we look at that mosaic, we might be able to discern a pattern. Nothing has made there be a pattern. It is as if the mosaic tiles had been placed in a bucket, shaken up, and then thrown out on the floor. But even if nothing but pure chance has made the tiles land where they have, there still can be a discernible pattern. It could be, as a matter of fact, that whenever there is a blue mosaic tile, there is a red one next to it. Nothing makes this be the case. Nothing compels or necessitates it. It's just a fact about the mosaic.

The mosaic is an analogy but it is useful. Instead of types of tile, the world consists of types of event, according to Humeans. And our beliefs about causation are determined simply by discovering such patterns in nature. The analogy might illuminate certain features of causation, such as its apparent asymmetry. By the asymmetry of causation, we mean that A causes B but B does not cause A, whatever A and B are. So striking a match causes it to light, rather than vice versa. For a Humean, this just means that A is always followed by B but B is not always followed by A. This is perfectly possible, as the mosaic shows. We said that whenever there is a blue tile, there is a red one next to it. But this does not entail that whenever there is a red tile there is a blue one next to it. There could be some lonely red tiles surrounded by tiles of other colours. We said only that the blue tiles will always be accompanied by red ones.

We saw in the quotation from Hume that he said there is only conjunction, never connection. Hume's view is often called a constant conjunction account. For A to cause B is for there to be a constant conjunction between A and B (plus a few other

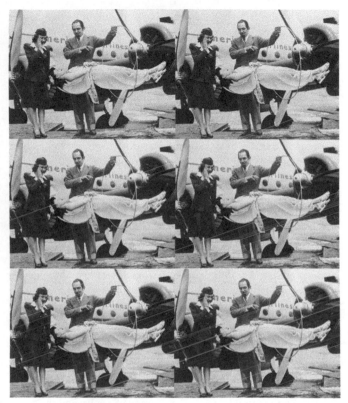

2. Regularity without production?

conditions, which will be discussed in the next chapter). Now
constant conjunction seems like a very simple idea. Perhaps it is
too simple. But Humeans will point out that no matter how
sophisticated or technical is the case at hand, the assumption of
causation still comes down to there being a constant conjunction
between cause and effect.

It seems clear that beheading causes death. For our Humean,
this means nothing more than that all beheadings have been

followed by the death of the subject. Now one might be tempted to say that this is more than just a constant conjunction. There is, one might protest, a very good reason why death follows beheading. The brain controls many functions of the body through a mechanism of nerves in the spinal cord. If this is severed, the organism can no longer function. But Humeans have an answer to this view. Although we often believe there to be a mechanism that is responsible for a constant conjunction or regularity, the workings of this mechanism themselves can only be explained in terms of further regularities. Thus, it is nothing more than a regularity that once a spinal cord is severed, several bodily functions cease. So the existence of mechanisms does not show us that Hume was wrong to think that causation was only regularity. These mechanisms 'work' in the same way: they will offer us just more regularities.

To take another, very mundane, case from domestic plumbing: whenever you pull the flush handle on the toilet, water is released from the cistern down into the bowl. Here there is a constant conjunction. It looks to be no accident. There is an explanation, which you find when you look inside the cistern. Pulling down the handle lifts the flush valve, allowing all the water through a pipe leading to the bowl. But all we have found, according to Hume (though he never actually wrote about water closets), is a further constant conjunction between the opening of a valve and the movement of water. Maybe there are further explanations of this constant conjunction—in terms of vacuums and gravity—but once again these explanations can rest ultimately on nothing more than constant conjunctions. It is another regularity that water fills a vacuum and that it flows downhill.

No matter how detailed and sophisticated our causal case is, it must always resolve into regularity, a Humean will claim. And this seems to be supported when we consider the ultimate, fundamental laws of nature. By fundamental, we can mean simply that there is no further explanation. Consider the law of gravitational attraction, for instance. Assuming this really is fundamental, then all we can say about it is that every object released near the surface of the Earth has fallen towards it. More generally, objects move towards each other with a force as described in the gravitational attraction law (that is, as a function of their masses and distance apart). The maths can be fancy, but the basic idea is that the laws of nature are just summaries or systematizations of the regularities that occur in the world.

A headache for Humeans

Hume's account may be thought plausible as an explanation of our current beliefs about what causes what. We may have seen many cases where those with headaches feel better soon after taking paracetamol. And this might lead us to think, on the basis of that regularity, that paracetamol cures headaches.

But what should a Humean with a headache do? Should they take the pill? Hume accepts that human beings think in a certain way. Our minds form habits of thought and it is quite natural that, having seen others (and ourselves on previous occasions) get better from taking a pill, we should do so on the next occasion we get a headache. But there is no rational basis for deciding to do this, in Hume's philosophy. It is natural for humans to form expectations that the future will be like the past, and Hume's main work was called *A Treatise of Human Nature*, but this natural inference of thought has no rational justification.

A Humean should say, therefore, that while they will take the pill in the expectation that their headache will then cease, this is not a rational act because they believe there to be no real connection between paracetamol and pain relief.

The problem here is that our experience of regularities can only be of what is regular thus far. In cases we have observed, A has been followed by B; but given that nothing about A makes B occur—it's just a fact that it has done so—then there is no rational justification for saying that in the future As will be followed by Bs.

To put this in more philosophical terms, Hume's account of causation invites the problem of inductive scepticism. Induction is a form of inference we arguably draw from past observed cases to future unobserved cases. Having seen matches light when struck, one assumes future struck matches will light. The regularity view offers us no explanation of why this should be, however, so the inductive inference looks to be entirely groundless. Hume was not happy with this implication, but he thought it inescapable.

Any time, any place, anywhere

Modern-day proponents of Humeanism, such as the aforementioned David Lewis, see the Humean mosaic in a slightly different way, concerned more with the metaphysical whole of reality rather than just our temporal perspective on it. When such modern metaphysicians speak of the regularities, they think of the regularities to be found in all the world's events, from start to finish, omnitemporally.

If we consider our Humean mosaic again, we would be urged by Lewisians to think of it as a mosaic showing all the events that occur at any place and any time. What count as genuine regularities are those that are constant conjunctions throughout all of history, from the Big Bang to the Big Crunch, if these are the world's first and final events. As historically situated human beings, we might be unlucky if something looks like a regularity but is not really so. It may be in the history of the world that until this year, every A was followed by a B, and we might assume A to cause B, but from next year A is not very often followed by B.

The world will have been unkind to us if it misleads us in this way. But for all genuine causes, the future instances will be like the past. They will be the ones that have genuine constant conjunction every time. The problem of induction just relates to our knowledge, therefore, and our limited perspective on the world. It is not a problem of causation itself, on this omnitemporal version of Humeanism.

But perhaps this only draws attention to a further problem for the regularity theory. Whether one event causes another, on this view, is not just a matter concerning those two events and how they relate. For one to be the cause of the other depends on what happens at other places and times. According to the omnitemporal Humean view, it depends on every such instance of the first event being followed by the second. Causation thus becomes a hugely relational matter.

We might think that when one billiard ball collides with another, then it is that very collision with that very one ball that makes that object ball move away. What does it matter what happens on the next billiard table? How can the events over there affect what happens on your billiard table? However, whether this white ball caused the red one to move is, according to Humeanism, dependent on every other collision of balls in the whole history of the world, presumably including some that occur a thousand years later. So, in general, A causes B only relative to many other events. Can this really be so?

A distinction is sometimes drawn between this relational kind of view and singularist accounts of causation. A singularist is looking for causal connections between individual dated events: such as John's clapping of his hands at midday on Thursday causing a distinctive sound. Singularists think that we can ignore everything else but these two events, if all we want to know is whether one caused the other.

In contrast, Humeans are effectively claiming, as an essential part of their theory, that one thing causes another only if that sequence is an instance of a covering law. There have to be general causal laws, such as that food nourishes (or, rather, consumption of food is always followed by nourishment) in order for it to be the case that Jane's eating of this loaf of bread causes her to be nourished. And this idea is not without its attractions. It is not as if anything can go about causing any other thing, willy-nilly. If there were no regular pattern in what followed what, wouldn't we indeed have little reason to believe in causation?

Accidents will happen

There is, however, a further weakness of a constant conjunction view that opponents have claimed. Arguably, the theory has no resources to distinguish between causes and coincidences. Should there really be no possible distinction between regularities that are genuinely causal and those that are merely accidental?

We tend to distinguish coincidences from causal cases. Winning a bet at the races while wearing one's lucky tie might be one such coincidence. Surely the tie cannot affect the outcome of the race. But what if the same outcome occurs the next time one places a bet while wearing the tie? And again?

What would a Humean say about the causes–coincidences distinction? What they would have to do is look at the wider pattern of events: whether events of the first type are constantly conjoined with events of the second type. And here we are not entitled to make any presumptions about what is a coincidence. Within Humeanism, any two types of events could be constantly conjoined (and any two types might not be constantly conjoined). In other words, causality is, on this view, an entirely contingent relation. There is no contradiction in any two distinct types of event either being causally related or not being causally related.

But here is the problem. When someone wins at the races while wearing a lucky tie, we naturally think of it as just a coincidence. But suppose they won each and every time they wore it? The

Humean would have to say, consistently with their theory, that since causation consists just in regularity, the lucky tie caused each time the winning of the bet.

We might think that it would be unlikely that one thing would follow another many times if it were just pure coincidence. That may be true but Humeans cannot really assert it. Hume has painted himself into a corner where he has to say that if A is always followed by B then A causes B. The theory implies this. Non-Humeans, on the other hand, could leave it an open question. In all those cases where A is regularly followed by B, for any A and B, some will be cases of genuine causation—perhaps most of them—but some could be accidental. The non-Humean has at least the conceptual resources to distinguish causes and coincidences and it appears that the Humean does not very easily. A more sophisticated form of Humeanism would be required if it is to make this distinction.

How regular is regular?

If one thinks about the issue of causes and coincidences, it brings to light a seemingly paradoxical result of the Humean regularity theory. It will be easier for an accidental constant conjunction to occur the fewer instances it has. If A occurs only five times in the history of the world, and is followed by B on each such occasion, then it counts as an exceptionless regularity. But it seems quite possible, given the few instances, that it could be a mere coincidence that the Humean mistakes for a cause. The Humean has to concede that regularity, hence causation, is more likely the fewer instances there are of the cause. This seems paradoxical because we usually would think it more likely that A is a cause of B the more instances there are of A followed by B.

There is an extreme version of this problem. What if there is only a single instance of A? For example, suppose there is a universe that contains only two events: there is a bang and then there is a flash.

Now the question is: Did the bang cause the flash? If one follows a constant conjunction account, it seems that one has to say yes. The bang was always, in every case (in that one) followed by a flash. But we still might say that it could be a mere coincidence.

It should be added in fairness to Hume that he has an answer to this kind of objection. In discussing whether God could have caused the existence of the universe, in an act of creation, he argues that this could never count as causation. The reason is that this is an entirely unique event—certainly occurring only once—and, he insists, it is repetition that makes us form our idea of cause. So for Hume to believe that God caused the universe, he would want to see him do it multiple times. Hume does not say exactly how many times is enough, but the general idea is that we should become more persuaded that causation has occurred the more instances of its conjunction we see, rather than the fewer instances we see. That certainly seems a judgement on his part that coheres with common sense.

We now have the basics in place of a Humean regularity view. More detail is to be added. We will see that regularity is not quite all that we need in order to say that one thing causes another. But regularity is a major part of the notion of cause. And it has to be conceded that in many sciences we are mainly searching for correlations. If a trial shows that recovery rate from an illness improves when a certain drug is taken, isn't that enough for us to think that some causation is at work?

Those working in the sciences are sometimes discouraged from asking the question of whether there is 'real' causation behind the correlation. Perhaps it is more than suspicion of metaphysics that is behind this. Perhaps there is also a view that correlation is all there is. We should not expect anything lurking behind it, producing the regularity. We will see, however, that there are a number of other issues to be addressed and other theories of causation that might prove more attractive.

Chapter 3
Time and space: do causes occur before their effects?

Hume realized that there was more to our idea of causation than merely correlation. That two phenomena were regularly conjoined would not alone be enough to give us an idea of cause. Whenever a child is born, for instance, we know that it is correlated with an egg being fertilized, usually after intercourse. But the child's birth did not cause the intercourse. That gets things the wrong way round.

Two more ideas were involved, thought Hume. In addition to constant conjunction, Hume thought that our notion of cause included the ideas of temporal priority and contiguity. Temporal priority means that causes must precede their effects in time. Contiguity means that causes and effects must be at places next to each other. There is intuitive appeal in the idea that both temporal priority and contiguity are needed for an idea of cause. But we will see that not only can both be challenged, but the two conditions are also in tension: one undermines the other.

We should bear in mind that Hume's account of causation occurs in a context of empiricist epistemology. His concern is with what our idea of a cause is, and where it came from. If we can show no original sense impression or series of such impressions from which we got an idea, then he thinks it is illegitimate and should be rejected.

This raises all sorts of questions of philosophical interpretation: about whether we can know of anything other than our own experiences. There are, though, some important metaphysical questions to ask about causation too, which are not just questions about our concept of cause.

First things first

What is so appealing about temporal priority? Our experience seems to show us that causes come first, and effects some time after. The match is first struck and then it lights; the drug is taken and then the headache goes; the libel is first made and then the reputation is harmed; sugar is placed in tea and then it dissolves; a rivet loosens and then the structure collapses much later. And from this, we can use the temporal ordering of events to distinguish the causes from the effects when there is a regularity.

Suppose we were to find that happy people tend to be friendly. There is a correlation between happiness and friendliness. We might decide that there is a causal connection between these two factors, but which was the cause and which was the effect? A sensible way of settling this would be to investigate which comes first. Were these people happy first and then became friendly? Or were they first friendly and then became happy? This wouldn't quite settle the matter conclusively, but it could be a good guide.

One might also look at it this way. Suppose in law that a manufacturer is accused of making a number of their employees ill through exposure to some substance without adequate protection. What better a defence could the company produce than if they could show that each employee had the illness to the same severity before starting work for the company? If the alleged effect did not come after the alleged cause, then it seems to automatically rule out causation.

When we accept that causes are temporally prior to their effects, something useful comes out of it. If A caused B, then B did not cause A. The acceptance of temporal priority might explain this asymmetry. If A caused B, and causes must be prior to their effects, then it follows that A is before B. It follows again that B cannot, therefore, be before A; and thus that B cannot be a cause of A.

Temporal priority would deliver an asymmetry to causation that neither constant conjunction nor contiguity could. We are yet to examine contiguity but constant conjunction wouldn't do the job for the following reason. While A being constantly conjoined with B does not entail that B is constantly conjoined with A, it does not exclude it either. It is possible, for instance, that everyone who is happy is friendly but also that everyone who is friendly is happy. Technically speaking, we would classify constant conjunction as a non-symmetric relation (a symmetric relation is one that if A holds it to B, then B has to hold it to A, such as where A is the same height as B).

This asymmetric temporal priority seems very important to our notion of causation. It adds something crucial to regularity. It gives it a direction. Let us now turn to contiguity.

Matching causes to effects

Hume's view was that if A and B are constantly conjoined and A occurs before B, then this still would not be enough for us to conclude that A is a cause of B. The reason for this is that A and B would also need to be next to each other; that is, spatially adjacent. This is what Hume means by contiguity.

Let us consider a mundane example once more. We can assume that there is a regularity between matches being struck and matches lighting. We have now added that in order for us to say that the striking of the match caused it to light, we should say that the striking occurred before the lighting. But what is to rule out the following fancy scenario? Suppose three matches are struck at the same time, one in Norway, one in the UK, and one in Spain. All of them light shortly after, and in each case the striking occurred before the lighting. But why do we not take seriously the suggestion that the striking of the match in Norway caused the Spanish match to light, the striking of the match in Spain caused the UK match to light, and the striking of the UK match caused the Norwegian match to light?

Hume has an answer to this. We think that causation does not occur over a distance: not immediately so, in any case. The cause of the lighting—being struck against a rough matchbox—must be at the same place as the lighting. Similarly, for one billiard ball to cause another to move, it must touch it: it must occupy the next available place to the ball it moves. And for someone to become ill from a bacterium, the bacterium must come into contact with them. You cannot strangle someone without touching them; and you cannot be nourished by food at a distance.

One thing leads to another

One might think that there are some easy counterexamples to Hume's principle of contiguity. There can be at least some action at a distance. Suppose Peter sees Jane at the other end of the street and calls to her. She turns and sees him. Peter has affected Jane over a distance. An earthquake in Italy could be felt in Germany; the burning Sun 93 million miles away can warm the faces of Earth's inhabitants; reading of suffering in a distant country can cause someone to shed a tear; and a crop famine in a particular continent can raise food prices on the other side of the world. Why are these not genuine examples of action over a distance?

In all such cases, it seems plausible that the cause works on the effect via a chain of intermediate causes and effects, where each such link in the chain involves contiguous action. The earthquake in Italy shakes an area of land, for instance, that moves the contiguous area of land, which in turn moves the next contiguous area, and so on until the shocks reach Germany. And the Sun sends its rays through space, passing through all the intermediate locations on the way to Earth. It does not pass straight from one to the other. Similarly, the suffering in a distant country was seen by someone there, who wrote about it. Someone decided to publish it and distribute it to other places. In each such case, we can find that causation has travelled from one place to a distant one only by effects at each of the intervening points. Even when Peter calls to Jane, the sound—vibrations in the air—disturbs also the places in between Peter and Jane.

The idea of the causal chain is an important one. Causes can line up in a row and follow one after another, creating effects at a much later time and distant place. One very simple way of picturing it is what happens when we line up dominoes, stood on their ends no more than a domino's length apart. You topple the

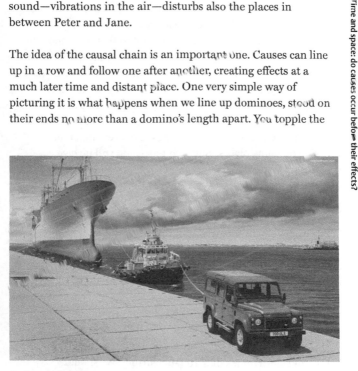

3. **A causal chain**

first, knocking it into the second, and they all fall in turn. It is easy to do this and fun to watch: fun because we get to see an extended causal chain play out. The knocking of the first domino causes the falling of the last one, some time later and some distance away. We can see how it does so through a series of individual causal transactions.

Chains are often used in causal explanations. As in the domino case, we can see that one thing led to another. Sometimes finding an originating cause is more illuminating than discovering what was the immediately preceding cause. What caused World War II immediately was Chamberlain's issuing of an ultimatum that was ignored. But what led to Chamberlain issuing such an ultimatum is more illuminating: Nazi aggression against Germany's neighbours. There is a story of how we got to that point too. The standard account in history is that Archduke Franz Ferdinand was assassinated in Sarajevo, leading to the outbreak of World War I. The settlement of that war produced the Treaty of Versailles, the harshness of which upon Germany led to the rise of an expansionist movement of National Socialism. Causal chains can thus be spread over decades, centuries, and even millennia, reaching far-flung places. But each link could still involve contiguity and immediate temporal priority.

Right place, right time

While we saw that there was an intuitive appeal to the notion that causes must precede their effects, it also raises a problem. How can a cause affect something unless it exists at the same time as the thing it affects? For someone to catch a cold, the virus must exist at the same time as that person and come into contact with them. And for one billiard ball to push another, they must both exist.

Let us consider Hume's billiard table further. We should remember that Hume advocates the temporal priority of cause over effect and that he also calls the billiard ball case the perfect instance of causation. One would think, then, that the example supports Hume's claim of temporal priority.

But does it? If two balls collide, and one causes the other to move, when does the causation occur? Hume would account for the example as follows. First the cue ball rolls along the table, before the object ball moves. Second, the two balls touch. And, third, the object ball moves away from the point of collision. If we take the cause to be the rolling of the cue ball, and the effect to be the rolling of the object ball, it would seem to support Hume's claim that causes precede their effects. But is this the right way to understand the case?

No causation occurs until the cue ball meets the object ball. We know this because we could stop the cue ball with our hands at any point until it reaches the collision and it will not have affected the object ball at all. It is not until they touch that any causation occurs with respect to the object ball. And we know this from Hume's other principle: contiguity. The cue ball cannot affect the object ball at a distance and, thus, the rolling of the ball prior to the collision becomes somewhat of an irrelevance. That is just the story of how the cue ball got to the point of collision. The contiguity condition tells us that the causation occurs with the touching of the cause and effect. And given that this happens at a distinct moment in time, or slightly extended period of time, then it suggests that the cause cannot occur before the effect. The demands upon causation of both temporal priority and contiguity seem to be in tension, therefore.

That argument seems enough to challenge the intuition that causes must occur before their effects but it is worth noting that we can run a similar argument in relation to a view that effects must occur after their causes. Once the object ball starts moving away, someone could stop it with their hand and interrupt its motion. But that wouldn't mean that the cue ball had not caused it to do something. Indeed, any causation with respect to the action of the cue ball seems to be over and done once the two balls part. The cue ball cannot affect the object ball once it has moved away until they clash again at some other time. What happens to it after it has run away is just the story of what happens to it after the cue ball has caused it to move.

This suggests that the causation between the cue ball and object ball occurs at the time that they are touching, where momentum is being passed from one to the other. It cannot occur before they meet nor after they have parted, in accordance with the demand of contiguity.

Simultaneity

The foregoing discussion is a challenge to Hume's claim that causes must precede their effects. Hume seemed to think that this was part of the very concept of cause. But, if he is wrong, what could we say instead? An option, suggested by the billiard case, is to say that causes and effects are simultaneous. This would allow us to retain Hume's other commitment, to contiguity.

Immanuel Kant (1724–1804), a philosopher following Hume, thought the idea of simultaneous causation to be a credible one. His example concerned a ball resting on a cushion, which caused the cushion to deform whenever it was there, and would cease doing so once it was removed. The ball acts upon the cushion over exactly the same interval of time that its effect occurs. And the billiard ball example is not too dissimilar to this. The balls do not touch for only an instant. Because they are less than perfectly rigid, they touch for a short period of time during which they deform slightly into each other and then spring away. This is when the momentum is passed from one to another. Or consider a house of playing cards. Two cards lean against each other, each simultaneously keeping the other up. If either is removed, the other falls down.

We can consider another case according to this model. An apparent example of temporal priority was that sugar being placed in a liquid (the cause) occurred before its dissolving (the effect). But we said in the case of the billiard balls that the rolling of the cue ball towards the point of impact was not really the cause but only the story of how the ball got to the point of impact. Similarly, no dissolving is occurring while the sugar cube is being held in someone's hand, being moved towards a cup of tea, for instance. The causation with respect to the dissolving of sugar occurs only once the sugar is in the tea. Someone placing it in the cup is just the explanation of how it got there. It's not really the cause of it dissolving. As soon as the sugar and tea are in contact, the causation begins. It is a process that takes time, unless it is somehow interrupted, and the causation will occur whenever there remain solid sugar and unsaturated liquid. The process takes time, but cause and effect seem to be there—simultaneous—throughout.

Now Hume had said, of course, that temporal priority was part of the very notion of cause. If he was right on this, we could not even entertain the idea of simultaneous causation. It would be like a contradiction in terms. But given that the examples mentioned above look perfectly coherent, then it seems more likely that Hume was wrong. Simultaneous causation is at least conceivable and some of these examples suggest it is even actually the case. And to reinforce the point, some find backwards time travel to be conceivable and that would suggest that causes could occur after their effects.

Suppose a time traveller appears in a time machine in 1974 but his appearance was caused by him flicking a switch in his time machine in 2074. Again, this seems conceivable, even if it is a fancy of science fiction, so Hume might be wrong that temporal priority of cause over effect is essential to causation. It is worth pointing out, however, that the argument for the simultaneity of cause and effect—that both must exist at the same time in order for one to affect the other—works against any temporal division of cause and effect, no matter what the direction of causation. The real problem in the time travel case seems to be the jump straight from one time to another.

Even if simultaneity is conceivable, that's not enough to guarantee that causation works that way, however. What, for instance, of the extended causal chains? If the assassination of Archduke Ferdinand in 1914 caused the eventual rise of National Socialism in Germany, much later, then there looks to be no case for simultaneity.

There are a number of possible replies. One would be to say, as Kant did, that some causation is simultaneous but not all is. Another Kantian thought is to make a distinction between instantaneous and simultaneous causation. Just because causes and effects can occur simultaneously does not mean that they occur instantaneously. Some causes have their effect over a lengthy period of time. Kant gave the example of a stove gradually heating a room.

While the assassination of Archduke Ferdinand may still be having its effect, however, it seems implausible to say that the cause is still present. The assassination was over in a flash. But what one might say is that each link in a causal chain involves only simultaneity of cause and effect, some of which involve temporally extended processes. The chain can thus take time. And the end point of each link in the chain could overlap with the next link in the chain, existing at the same time as its neighbour. Some such account might reconcile simultaneity with temporally extended causal chains.

Non-locality

We should not assume that Hume's notion of contiguity goes unchallenged either. Again, there's an argument that he was wrong to insist upon it as a conceptual truth.

Physicists discuss cases of quantum entanglement. This is where the properties of two particles look connected, such that a measurement on one seems to guarantee the outcome of a measurement on the other. What is challenging about the case is that this holds immediately and irrespective of distance. Allegedly, when the one particle is measured, then its entangled partner, no matter how far away, must have a certain value at that very moment.

Philosophers of physics are still trying to interpret exactly what is going on in these cases but one interpretation that is still entertained is that quantum entanglement involves instantaneous action over a distance, without any intermediate chain. This would be deeply puzzling because it seems to involve causation travelling faster than the speed of light, which is supposedly the fastest of all things.

Apart from that, however, what is significant is that it seems we are able to conceive of causation occurring non-locally, that is, without contiguity. Some call this the quantum non-locality of causation. Others call it spooky action at a distance. Whether it is a case of real causation remains to be confirmed, but it may tell us about our notion of cause nevertheless.

So both temporal priority and contiguity can be challenged. We might, however, still recall the reasons why Hume thought temporal priority and contiguity were needed. Constant conjunction would not be enough, he thought. How would we distinguish the cause from the effect? And how can we tell when we have genuine causes if we have nothing but regularity to go on? These are still good questions and anyone who rejects Hume's answers will have to find better ones of their own.

Chapter 4
Necessity: do causes guarantee their effects?

A common anti-Humean thought about causation is this. When causation is in play, the effect is more than just a mere possibility among many others. There is a good reason why the specific effect is produced. Causes, it is thought, compel or make their effects happen. When sugar is in hot tea it must dissolve; when a ball is kicked it must move; and when an organism has a certain gene structure, it must develop in a certain way.

What many think is lacking from a regularity view of causation, even if accompanied by the further requirements of contiguity and temporal priority, is a sense of the necessity of causes. The effect is no accident, given the occurrence of the cause. Instead, the cause is considered entirely sufficient for the effect to occur. Hume's philosophy, it is thought by many, contains too much contingency. The Humean mosaic suggests that, in theory, anything could follow anything. But anti-Humeans reject this. They argue for realism about causation, which they take to mean that causes are genuinely productive of their effects in a stronger sense than Hume allows.

What do we mean by necessity and contingency? Philosophers have different ways of conceptualizing these two options. By necessity, they may mean that something is strictly entailed, that it has to be the case, or that it is true in all possible worlds. By contingent, they may mean something that could be true or not, that it might be the case, or that it is true in some but not all possible worlds. It may be thought necessary that 2 + 2 = 4 but contingent that Oslo is the capital of Norway. Norway could, in theory, have chosen Tromsø as their capital city, but there is no possibility at all that 2 + 2 could not have equalled 4.

Other cases are controversial. Is it necessary or contingent that water is H_2O, that the speed of light is 186,000 miles per second in a vacuum, or that electrons are negatively charged? And within the debated category, we can also put causes. Is it necessary or contingent that water dissolves sugar, that paracetamol relieves pain, and struck matches light?

A matter of necessity?

Hume considered necessity as a possible fourth element to the idea of cause, alongside the three ideas we have already discussed: regularity, temporal priority, and spatial contiguity. He conceded that necessity was often part of the common understanding of cause. Philosophically, however, he concluded that it had no legitimate place.

His argument was that a single instance of causation did not reveal any evidence to us of necessity. Hume's view is that we just see a succession of events: one thing following another. Our idea of cause comes from seeing a repetition of the same kind of sequence of events. This forms in us an expectation that further cases will be like the ones we have seen. But there is no necessity that they be so. If a single case displays no necessity, then it can't come from just further instances of the same. Each case contains nothing but contingency; and no amount of further contingency ever gets us to necessity. That would be like hoping that additions of the number zero would eventually get us to one.

To make this less abstract, consider the striking of the match again. Hume says we see it struck and we see it light. The match might not have lit when struck. It could instead have evaporated. So while we see it light aflame, we cannot see that it had to light, of necessity. That is not part of our experience. And when we see more matches struck and lit, we are seeing just more of the same, where each individual striking also fails to reveal necessity. The Humean view is, then, that regularity fails to reveal any necessity in causation.

Real necessity, as far as Humeans are concerned, resides only in 'relations of ideas'; $2 + 2 = 4$ is necessary only because its truth is contained in the meanings of the ideas involved. Similarly, we can say that if today is Wednesday, tomorrow has to be Thursday. But the necessity of this truth is entirely in the words. There is no worldly necessity compelling the future.

A philosophical compulsion

Hume was arguing against a received view, one that we find in Aristotle and more recently in the likes of Baruch Spinoza (1632–77), who said of causation: 'From a given definite cause an effect necessarily follows' (Spinoza 1677, *Ethics* I, axiom III). Hume's argument is a powerful challenge to this idea but necessitarian views continue to resurface in contemporary metaphysics. Some take the laws of nature to be matters of absolute necessity, for instance, with causal sequences bound by them.

The attraction of the necessitarian view is that it takes seriously the feeling of compulsion in causation. Hume's contingentist view suggests that the effect could or could not occur. Nothing makes the effect happen, either way. But many cases suggest there is real necessity in effects. Everyone who has been beheaded, during the French Revolution for instance, has died. Do we really want to say that this is nothing more than a constant conjunction, and a matter of pure contingency? Or should we say that there is necessity? After all, there is surely no possibility that someone could survive once their head has been severed from their body.

The realist about causation—someone who thinks causation is a real thing—will reassert the view that Hume had tried to overturn. It is natural to think that the regularities in the world are there for a reason. Something makes it be the case that if you are beheaded you will die. And if there is some necessity in this then it will produce the constant conjunction. Regularity would thus be symptomatic of causation: a good way of identifying it.

The case for necessity in beheading looks strong. The necessitarian will say that the same is true of all other cases of causation. It seems hard to conceive of someone surviving without a head. While it seems easier to conceive of sugar being in a liquid without dissolving, isn't this just down to our relative ignorance of the true causes? If we knew enough about the processes involved, the argument would go, we would see that there is just as much inevitability in sugar dissolving in liquid as there is in someone dying when beheaded.

There remains the Humean challenge of how we could know from our experience that necessity was involved in any case of causation. A necessitarian might respond, however, that Hume's empiricist project is too restrictive over what counts as admissible evidence. Regularity might not strictly entail that there are real compelling causes at work. But perhaps the reality of causation is a plausible hypothesis—even the best explanation—of why there is so much regularity in nature. Maybe we think that Hume has set too high a standard of proof of the necessity of causes: a standard of proof that favours his own theory.

A necessitarian might also point out that their account has the advantage of explaining away the problems besetting Humeanism. Hume could not distinguish between accidental and genuinely causal constant conjunctions, for instance. But the realist about causation can indeed make that distinction. Some regularities will be mere coincidences; others necessitated causally. And if causation is a real thing, then it doesn't matter whether it has only a few instances, or perhaps just one instance. Whether it is real causation would not rest on how many instances it has. Nor need it be a relational view, so any singularist intuitions could be accommodated. Whether A causes B will not depend on events at other places and times but whether this specific A necessitated B.

There is a variation on the necessitarian view that respects the complexity of causal situations. Complexity is no doubt a pervasive feature of causal set-ups. Philosophers often try to abstract away from the details and we end up with discussions in which it looks like there is just one cause for every effect. Perhaps this is a harmless abstraction but only if there is nothing complexity brings to causation that we would miss if we try to ignore it.

John Mackie (1917–81) noted that for almost every effect, there could be multiple causes at work. Suppose someone drops a cigarette in a house, which subsequently burns down. The house is unlikely to have burnt down just from the dropping of the cigarette. It also needed the presence of flammable materials, such as furniture, and plenty of oxygen so that the flame could take hold. The dropped cigarette was not sufficient on its own to cause the fire but it certainly was an essential part of the whole cause of it. In other words, there would not have been a fire without the cigarette.

Furthermore, this whole set of factors, while being sufficient for the fire, was not itself necessary for it. The fire could have been caused in some other way, such as from an electrical fault. The set of factors was thus not necessary but nevertheless sufficient for the fire. We can thus venture what it is to be a cause in the following way:

[a cause] is an *insufficient* but *non-redundant* part of an *unnecessary* but *sufficient* condition [for the effect]: it will be convenient to call this (using the first letters of the italicized words) an *inus* condition. (Mackie, *The Cement of the Universe*, 1980: 62)

We commend this *inus*-condition account for recognizing causal complexity, to which we will return. But we also classify it as a sophisticated form of necessitarianism. To say that a set of causes, S, is sufficient for an effect is another way of saying that S necessitates it. These are just two different ways of saying that if S occurs, its effect must occur.

Free will

One reason why causation interests us is because it is related to the important issue of human agency. When we act, we cause things to happen. We are the originators of new causal chains, or so we would like to think. Causation is not merely a theoretical problem, which concerns only philosophers; nor is it important just because some distant discipline depends on it. Rather, if human agency is causation, then the issue is one of immediate significance to every being who has ever done anything.

A source of resistance to the necessitarian view of causation is, however, that it could threaten our free will. If causes necessitated their effects, then how would we escape the inevitability in the world? Wouldn't everything be determined and human beings would just be slaves to necessity, like everything else? This is the view known as determinism.

The idea of determinism needs more explanation. Suppose that every event that occurs is caused by other events, and causes necessitate their effects. And let us also suppose that human beings are subject just as much to causation as everything else. Causes act upon us, and thereby compel us to do things. And even if we decide to perform some action, then this must have been necessitated by

4. How free are we?

other causes, even if to us it appears spontaneous. What we think of as our own instigation of an action is itself just part of a preceding causal chain of events that we could not escape.

Determinism looks, therefore, to be a threat to our free will. Someone might decide that they want to go out and buy chocolate. But if that decision was caused by other events outside that person—causes that necessitated the decision—then in what sense is it truly free?

Some think that a way out of this problem is to distinguish between ordinary event causation and the sort of causing that agents do. The latter can be called agent causation. Perhaps if our minds are spirits or souls, then they might not be bound by the regular causation of the purely physical world. But such a response still faces a problem. Our bodies at least are physical things and it would thus seem hard to explain how they could escape the necessitation of standard event causation. What use is it then for your mind to make free decisions if the actions of your body are necessitated through causation?

However, it should be said that not everyone accepts determinism, allowing instead that there is at least some contingency in the world. Perhaps some events are uncaused. Or perhaps, as Humeans insist, causation doesn't involve necessity but allows complete contingency.

But here is one major problem. Just as necessity seems to impinge on our freedom, so too does contingency. Suppose your action is uncaused, or has some contingent element such as chance or randomness. That doesn't seem to make you free. On the contrary, it makes you lose control. You would now be a slave to chance instead of a slave to necessity. You don't want decisions to just pop into your head, as a matter of contingency: you want to retain power over them. There seems to be no free will if all is necessary; but no free will if all is contingent either.

It might seem easy to give up on human freedom at this point. We don't want to do so, however. The conclusion is still driven by a certain understanding of causation and we have not yet completed our survey of all theories. The issue of free will shows that the stakes are high. If our theory of causation forces us to give up human freedom, then perhaps there is something wrong with the theory.

Additive and subtractive interference

While appreciating the need for a causal connection that is stronger than constant conjunction—and thus the need for something that is non-Humean—there are nevertheless reasons why necessity seems to go too far.

Anyone who has struck a match knows that there are occasions when it fails to light. Sometimes this is because it has not been struck fast enough or in the right way. But at other times the correct technique may well have been utilized and the match still did not light. Suppose a gust of wind comes just at the time of the striking. It seems that there can be failures of causation, not because something is missing from the causal set-up, but because something else has been added, such as a gust of wind or water. And even if we protect the match from the wind or water, there could still also be some further factor that gets in the way of it lighting.

The world is regular and predictable, but it is less than perfectly so. It may be regular enough for us to know what we should try to do to bring about certain effects, but we also know that it is quite possible for our expectation to be disappointed.

Occasionally a fragile glass is dropped but somehow manages to survive the impact. Perhaps the glass fell in a certain way, landing on its strongest point. Or perhaps it luckily fell on a small soft part of the floor. And we know that while we try to build reliable machines, something can always go wrong with them. They could then fail to have the regular effect that they would normally have.

There are two ways in which a machine, or any kind of causal set-up, can fail. One would be if a part failed. Suppose a vital cog falls out of the machine, for instance, leaving a gap in the mechanism. The chain of causes that travels through the machine fails at that point. This is an instance of what we could call subtractive interference, which is the taking away of something from the cause, which prevents it having its usual effect.

In the second kind of case, we leave all parts of the machine intact but now we add some further element. Perhaps the cog in the machine gets covered in dust, which causes it to jam. Again the machine fails: not because something has been taken away but because something has been added. We will call this additive interference.

The possibility of additive interference is a threat to the necessitarian view of causation, and Hume realized this. When we say that one thing, A, necessitates another, B, then as necessity is usually understood, that would mean that whenever A occurs B must occur. This seems to follow in other cases of necessity. If today is Wednesday, tomorrow will always be Thursday. If it's Wednesday and it's July, then tomorrow is still Thursday; if it's Wednesday and Barack Obama is president, then tomorrow is still Thursday, and so on for anything else we can add.

So if we want to know whether one thing, A, necessitates another, B, we would want to know whether if there is A plus some other thing, X, for any X we care to name, there is still B. This is a test we could adopt for judging whether causes necessitate their effects. John Stuart Mill (1806–73) acknowledged this in the following passage:

> This is what writers mean when they say that the notion of cause involves the idea of necessity. If there be any meaning which confessedly belongs to the term necessity, it is unconditionalness. That which is necessary, that which must be, means that which will be whatever supposition we make with regard to other things. (Mill, *A System of Logic*, 1843: III, v, 6)

Now if it is possible to have additive interference, causation fails the test for necessity. We could have the usual cause of a certain effect and add something else—something as little as dust—and the effect fails to occur. It could also fail because someone throws a spanner in the works, a black hole appears, the causal mechanism falls down a sink hole, and so on. For all we know, the potential number of additive interferers is infinite. We cannot rule them all out in a finite list, insisting on their absence, for instance. In that case, how can we say that the cause necessitated the effect?

But is it really true that all cases of causation permit additive interferers? What of the case of beheading, for instance? That seems a good example of necessity. Surely there is nothing you could add that would allow you to survive? Well, that depends. There may be nothing at present, but survival after beheading is at least conceivable and it may just be a question of waiting for the development of adequate technology. In the TV show *Futurama*, for instance, a number of the characters are severed heads in sustaining jars of nutrients. Who's to say this is not a real possibility of additive interference? And if the head were able to send signals to its old body, perhaps that also could survive and move around on the owner's instructions.

This might seem like science fiction (which it is). But there was also a time when we thought people couldn't survive a minute without a heart. Today, heart transplant operations are fairly common and some even get mechanical parts installed. The question is whether the link between beheading and death, although it is clearly causal, is a matter of necessity. And it looks like it is not, even if everyone beheaded has died thus far.

The production process

The argument from additive interference has a broad significance. Even in those cases where a cause successfully produced its effect, it did not do so by necessitating it. There are some actual cases of failure of causation, due to additive interference; but even in the cases where there was no such interference, there could have been. No cause necessitates its effect, therefore, if the effect could have been prevented by an additional factor.

What this suggests is that, even for anti-Humeans, a distinction should be made between the notions of causal production and causal necessitation. Hume attacked necessity in causation and left in its place only pure contingency. If one thinks something is inadequate about his constant conjunction account, it doesn't follow automatically that one has to defend necessary connections in nature, as opposed to them residing only in 'relations of ideas'.

One might think that Hume is wrong and there is such a thing as genuine causal production over and above constant conjunction. But one need not defend what he had attacked: the notion of causal necessitarianism. Elizabeth Anscombe (1919–2001) challenged the claim that necessity was a part of our notion of causation. To say that A caused B, she argued, was not the same as to say that A necessitated B. The latter would have to be some supplementary thesis.

Anscombe's argument was based on the emergence of an increasingly respectable notion of indeterministic causation, which came to be taken seriously in 20th-century physics. It seems possible to have a case of causation that is probabilistic, which is not to say that it is completely random.

There may be a certain probability that a particle will have decayed after a certain period of time. There is nothing compelling it to have decayed by that time, and indeed it may not do so. But perhaps it is more likely to decay by that time than not. It has a propensity to do so. And when it does so, there seems no contradiction in the idea that the propensity caused the decay, even if it didn't guarantee it. A cause, then, could be something that raises the probability of an effect, and sometimes successfully produces it, but without ever ensuring it.

If we can make sense of a notion of indeterministic causation, then Anscombe was right that necessitation is not part of the concept of cause. Causal necessitarianism would be a supplementary thesis to the claim that there is genuine causal production. But even if necessitarianism is wrong, this still does not mean that we have to accept the completely contingent picture of the Humean mosaic. There could yet be other options.

Chapter 5

Counterfactual dependence: do causes make a difference?

Suppose a train gets delayed because there's an elk on the line. What warrants us saying that the elk caused the delay? We might not want to say that it is anything to do with regularity. For all we know, this is a singular instance and we don't know anything about what other elks are doing at other places and times. Our belief is about this particular elk causing a delay to this particular train at this particular time.

Here is a plausible thought. We might just say that had the elk not been on the line, the train would have run on time. Why does this sound plausible?

Causes, we might say, make a difference to what happens. They are difference makers. Without a particular cause occurring, history would have been different. President Lincoln was killed by an assassin's bullet, by which we mean that the gunshot caused his death. A way of understanding what this amounts to is that without the shot, Lincoln would have survived that trip to the theatre.

There are lots of other things that could have been otherwise but which did not make a difference to his death. Had he been watching a different play, for instance, he would still have died from the gunshot. And had it been on a different night of the week, there is no reason to think he would have survived. The one thing that made the difference to him living or dying was undoubtedly the gunshot.

In looking for the cause, therefore, and in saying what it is for something to be a cause, the suggestion is that we should look for a difference maker. And a way of thinking about this is to imagine what would have happened if such-and-such had not been there. Whether the elk on the line made a difference, therefore, comes down to whether the train would have arrived on time had the elk not been there. One might suspect that it would have been on time but for the elk blocking the way.

This is an attractive principle and one that is often used in law and in medicine as a test of causation. If one sues a company for damages, for instance, one would need to show that the subject of the suit made a difference. If one suffers an illness, one would have to show that one wouldn't have suffered it but for the subject's actions or negligence. Similarly, if someone is prosecuted for causing an accident, it has to be shown that the accident wouldn't have happened but for the actions or omissions of the defendant.

In philosophical terms, this would be known as a counterfactual dependence test of causation. And there is a philosophical theory that this is more than just a test: that causation itself consists in counterfactual dependence between events.

If things were different...

By counterfactual, we simply mean that which is contrary to the facts. So if it is a fact that there was an elk on the line, then it is a contrary-to-fact assumption that there was no elk there. We often like to entertain contrary-to-fact assumptions and consider what would have happened in those circumstances. What if Germany had won World War II? Would we all be speaking German? And what if aliens landed in London today, which we assume they will not? What difference would they make?

To get a theory of causation as a counterfactual dependence, we need to add more elements. First, we are speaking not just of a counterfactual assumption but also a dependence on that assumption. You might say that if the Sun goes out it will get very cold here, stating that one thing depends on the other. And you will probably be quite happy to grant this conditional true even if its antecedent (its 'if…' clause) is false. It being very cold here counterfactually depends on the Sun going out.

But that is not all. There can be counterfactual dependences that are not causal. If this month is June (which it's not), then you know that next month is July. Next month being July counterfactually depends on this month being June: but it's not caused by this month being June. Those who defend this as a theory of causation, therefore, need to distinguish those counterfactual dependences that are causal from those that are not.

One idea is that the counterfactual dependence has to be between separate events. Causation needs to be a natural relation, concerning events that are happening in the world, rather than what Hume called relations of ideas. Some counterfactual dependences will be purely logical, mathematical, or analytic (Hume's relations of ideas). Others will concern events and facts in the world depending on each other, and that is what interests us.

Relations and relata

Since Hume's work, it has been natural to think of causation as a relation between distinct events. A relation connects two or more things and a question for the theory of causation is what those things are. Humeans tend to say that they are events whereas Aristotelians tend to think of them as substances: individual objects, for instance.

An Aristotelian would point out that it is the elk, an individual biological entity, that is causing the lateness of the train. A Humean, on the other hand, would say it is the event of the elk being on the rail that causes the event of the train being late. How one understands the relata of causal relations can thus be revealing of one's underlying ontological assumptions. If a philosopher speaks of the cause of a sugar lump's dissolving as *it being put in water*, then it might reflect a Humean basic framework.

The counterfactual dependence view of causation is usually thought of as another Humean view of causation. Hume's work has spawned two different theories of causation as he said things favourable to both. But what makes them both Humean is the idea that causation is a contingent relation between distinct events. The difference between the two theories is whether that relation is one of constant conjunction or counterfactual dependence. David Lewis, who gave us the notion of the Humean mosaic, is known as a supporter of the counterfactual dependence view. But that causation is a contingent relation between events—or even that it is a relation at all—is something that an anti-Humean might challenge.

Facts and counterfacts

What do we have in the case where the elk caused the train delay? Humeans say we have just one event followed by another. There is an elk on the line and the train is late. There is no strong connection between these two events. The elk does not make the train late, necessitate it, or even tend towards it. This might look even weaker than a regularity theory.

It is therefore the counterfactual dependence part of the theory that does the work. There are lots of cases where one event follows another. What makes some cases causal is that, in those, had the first event not occurred, the second would not have occurred either. So the difference between there being causation and there not being causation isn't found just in the facts—about what actually happens—but in truths about what would have happened if things were different.

Viewed this way, the theory sounds somewhat incredible. Causation seems to consist not in what there is, but in something that is not: something that is contrary to fact. One might think that the elk's presence actually affected some other thing: it got in the way of the train. But we can only say the elk caused the delay, on this account, if it is true that had it not been there, the train would have run on time.

All is not lost for the counterfactual dependence view, however. As long as we can give a credible account of what counterfactual truths consist in, then it is no drawback that the theory relies on them.

One view of counterfactuals is called fictionalism. The idea is that when one thinks of a counterfactual supposition, it is like one is considering a fiction. Given that the elk actually was on the line, then the situation in which it was not there at that time and place is a mere fiction. Just as we can entertain, enjoy, and understand the fiction that there was a boy called Oliver Twist who was sold from a workhouse and met a man called Fagin, so can we grasp easily the fiction of a certain elk being absent from a rail line.

But is this enough for a theory of causation? Oliver Twist is just a fiction. He has no existence other than in the minds of the author and his readers. A character in a novel surely cannot causally interact with real people and things outside the novel. Could the real facts of causation in our world come down to some such fiction? Given that it is merely a made-up supposition that there was no elk on the line, how could such a fiction possibly determine important real-world matters about what causes what?

The worry might be that a fictionalist account of counterfactuals leaves them with insufficient metaphysical clout to fix the very real causal facts. Perhaps, then, we could find a more substantial account, which gives counterfactual truths some real being.

David Lewis offers such an account, though it comes at a price. What is counterfactual in our world, he says, is factual in some other world. In our world there was an elk on the line and the train was late, but there is another world very similar to ours in which there was no elk on the line. This other world is as much like ours in every other respect except for there being no elk in the way of the train. And in such a world, Lewis maintains, the train runs on time.

For it to be true that if there had been no elk on the line, the train would have run on time, it is necessary that there is a world as similar as possible to ours in every other respect but for the elk, and in that world the train has no delay. This other world has as many of the same facts and laws of nature as our world as is possible, consistent with the elk being absent. We cannot assume any additional truth that is not also true in our world, such as that there is also a bear on the line. And given this, the theory goes, then without the elk we know that there is nothing else in the way of the train.

Lewis has made the counterfactual truths substantial: indeed, they are all actual truths relative to the worlds within which they are located. This allays the worry about fictionalist interpretations of counterfactuals. But it creates another worry. For Lewis's version of the theory to work, there must be a plurality of concrete other worlds—one for each possible situation—and each just as real as ours. Lewis is adamant that these worlds must be real in the full sense. We have already seen why. They have a substantial job to do. But this reality of many other real worlds is also seen by many as an ontological extravagance. We cannot say for sure that

5. A world for every possibility

there are no such worlds: and a reason for this is that worlds are spatiotemporally disconnected from each other. There is no interaction between worlds, so we cannot check empirically for their existence. This might nevertheless be thought too costly and counterintuitive for us to accept.

Testing counterfactuals

Before philosophers get too carried away with their imaginations, however, what about the simple idea that we could test whether a counterfactual is true? Instead of merely considering some other possible world in which the counterfactual supposition is true, what about if we make it true in our own world and then see what happens?

There must surely be some simple practical tests that we could perform if we want to understand what is causing what. We can intervene and manipulate the world.

Suppose you see a house of cards and assume that a card at the bottom is (in part) holding up some of the cards above it. You might then think that if that card was not there, the rest above it would come tumbling down, which seems to indicate causation. You may merely believe there to be this counterfactual dependence but you could of course just remove the bottom card and see if the rest do indeed fall. One might, of course, prefer not to do this. Testing this causal situation seems also to destroy it. But there is a similar case of testing counterfactuals that looks a lot more productive.

Suppose a new drug is invented and we want to know whether it has a positive causal effect on a certain disease. How do we find out? The medical profession has settled upon a standard test that looks remarkably like a counterfactual dependence test but without the ontological baggage of Lewis's concrete other worlds. The test is randomized controlled trial (RCT).

Test subjects are selected for a trial and then divided at random into two groups. If the numbers are large enough, and the division is genuinely random, then these groups should be pretty much alike. The trial drug is given to the first group, which we now call the treatment group. The other group gets just a placebo, unknown to them.

One possible outcome from such a trial is that the recovery rate among the treatment group is better than the recovery rate in the placebo group. This is when we would be tempted to make a causal claim: that the drug cures or controls the disease. The reason we would feel justified in saying this is because we think the placebo group shows that had the drug not been taken, fewer people would have recovered.

A key component that allows us to make this claim is the randomization that divided the two groups. We said that for Lewis's theory, the counterfactual world that one considers should be as similar to the actual world in as many respects as possible, consistent with the counterfactual supposition. Randomization over a sufficiently large sample should ensure that the two groups are similar: at least similar enough for our purposes. So if one group has a better recovery rate than another, it should not be merely because there are different types of people in one group from the other: more healthy people, for example. What this shows is that certainly in the medical profession, a counterfactual dependence test of causation is taken seriously.

Right way round?

It is one thing to use some sort of counterfactual dependence as a test of causation and another thing to say that causation consists in such dependence. The philosophical theory that we have been considering opts for the latter. It says that causation is nothing more than a counterfactual dependence between events.

One could argue, however, that this gets the order of explanation the wrong way round. The reason we might think that some events counterfactually depend on others is because they are causally connected. If we take the RCT case, you might say that there is a reason the treatment group has a better rate of recovery than the placebo group. It is not some basic, Humean fact; it's that the drug actually works. It has a causal effect. Wouldn't those people in the treatment group who recovered still have recovered from taking the drug, even if there was no placebo group? Suppose by administrative error they had forgotten to give that group their placebos. Surely that wouldn't have been relevant to the treatment group and whether they recovered or not. So how can whether the drug caused their recovery be determined by what happens to the placebo group, who don't interact in any way with the treatment group?

A criticism of Lewis's view is that it is our beliefs about the real causal connections at this world that inform our beliefs about what would happen at other worlds, where things were slightly different. After all, we cannot see into those worlds so there is no other evidence for our beliefs about them. Hence, we believe that if the elk had not been there, the train would have been on time, precisely because we believe in this world that the elk caused the delay.

The suggestion, then, is that the counterfactual dependence view gets it the wrong way round. Counterfactual dependence is not the reason why things are causally related; being causally related is the reason why some events have a counterfactual dependence. The latter might just be a product or symptom of causation.

Overdetermination

But is it even a symptom? Some critics have pointed out that there could be cases of causation without counterfactual dependence and also counterfactual dependence without causation.

What if, as well as there being an elk on the track, it is standing next to a faulty signal, stuck on red? In such a case, the train would be delayed even if there was no elk on the line. If the elk did not stop the train, something else would have. Here it seems as if the elk does cause the delay, but the train would still have been delayed even without the elk. The elk is a cause but not, it seems, a difference maker.

The reason this happens is that we have an overdetermination of the effect. Both the elk and the stuck signal are able to delay the train. But where we have overdetermination, there is no counterfactual dependence. If the elk had not been there, the train would still have been late because of the stuck signal. And if the signal had not been stuck, the train would still have been late because of the elk. So neither comes out as a cause of the delay if causation consists in counterfactual dependence.

Counterfactual dependence theorists have tried hard to show that overdetermination of effects cannot really happen. Perhaps one cause always comes before and pre-empts the other, such that one does all the causing while the other does none. But why is simultaneous overdetermination a possibility that we should rule out? Having two causes of an effect operating at the same time, each individually enough, seems a perfectly possible scenario. If the only motivation for ruling it out is that it saves the counterfactual dependence theory of causation, then it looks like an ad hoc move.

Without which not

Overdetermination is causation without counterfactual dependence. There is also the opposite case. There are some instances that do not seem causal but there is nevertheless a counterfactual dependence between distinct events. This sort of case is what we would call a *sine qua non* or necessary condition.

One afternoon, John increases the pace of his stride. He wouldn't have been able to do so unless he had got out of bed that morning. John increasing his pace thus counterfactually depends on him getting out of bed. But did his getting out of bed that morning cause him to increase his pace in the afternoon? It doesn't look like it. When John got up, he had no intention of increasing his walking pace later. But it was a necessary condition for it. He couldn't have been walking in the afternoon if he was still in bed. *Sine qua non* means *without which not*, which does not look to be the same as a causal connection.

Similarly, John's extra speed counterfactually depends on the Big Bang but arguably the Big Bang didn't cause it. It was merely a necessary condition for it. Your death counterfactually depends on your birth: indeed everything you ever do subsequently in your life will counterfactually depend on your birth. But did your birth cause all of those things? Did it cause you to choose pasta rather than pizza at the restaurant, to prioritize your friendships, to give up smoking, to move to London? Moreover, Hume becoming a philosopher counterfactually depended on him having great-grandparents. It is arguable, however, that his great-grandparents didn't cause him to become a philosopher, because they had no influence over his decision or education. Thought about this way, the gap between a necessary condition and a true cause looks to be quite wide. That would seem to indicate that counterfactual dependence cannot be the same as causation.

Chapter 6
Physicalism: is it all transference?

The accounts we have considered thus far have all been inspired by Hume and his project of reducing causation away to other conceptual terms. But there is another kind of approach that we could take. It is one thing to ask what we mean by the concept of cause; perhaps there is another question of what causation *is*.

John Locke (1632–1704) in his *An Essay Concerning Human Understanding* (1691) drew a famous distinction between nominal and real essence. The nominal essence of a thing—gold, for instance—was the set of superficial, observable qualities by which we recognized it. Gold is yellow, shiny, and malleable, we might say. And this nominal essence is what we use to identify gold and talk about it. But Locke thought things also had an underlying essence—the real essence—and it was this that was truly the thing. Locke thought the real essence was hidden but with advances in science we now think we know something about it. To be gold is to have atomic number 79, for example, which is to say that gold is the element that has 79 protons in its nucleus.

When we are considering what causation is, perhaps the key issue is to discover its real essence: what it is in the world rather than what our concept of cause is. After all, the common concept of cause might be a mess with there being no one single thing that everyone means when they use the term. Pluralists think this, as we shall see. Wouldn't it be rather fantastic if there was just one single and coherent thing that all people, in all places and eras, meant when they used the term cause? That would be a remarkable convergence of thinking, for which we humans are not famed. In that case, one might think a better approach would be to let some of the scientific experts tell us what causation is. It seems to be a physical phenomenon that ought to be the proper subject of empirical science to determine. Just as chemists took us away from the popular, rough, and inaccurate understanding of gold, shouldn't physicists investigate the world and tell us what causation really is?

Energetic scientists

What do we find when we look at the world, for the empirical evidence of causation? At one time we might have thought that causation was basically about objects bashing into each other and making others move. This idea was prominent during the age of mechanistic and corpuscularian philosophy. Corpuscularians thought that there were small parcels of matter, like tiny versions of Hume's billiard balls, that were also bashing each other around. The causal interactions we saw around us—at what we can call the macro level—were ultimately produced by the action of micro-level corpuscles.

We think we now have a better scientific understanding of the world but it is sometimes presented in ways that are structurally similar to the corpuscularian tradition. But now, instead of thinking of parcels of matter bashing into each other, we think of bundles of energy or other quantities being passed around. Conservation laws tell us that the quantity of energy in a system is stable but it can be passed around or transferred between regions.

This sounds abstract and technical but we can comprehend it in a relatively simple way. A billiard ball moves across the table

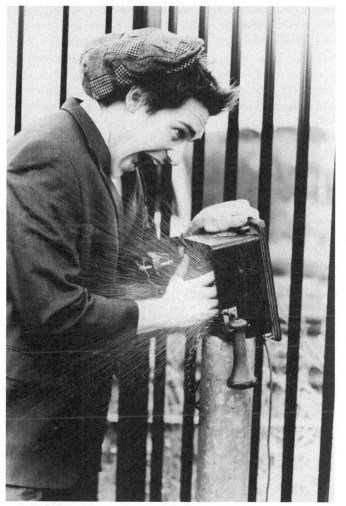

6. **Energy transference**

because it has momentum. This can be explained within physical theory in terms of energy, which we know is a function of mass and acceleration. When one ball collides with another, it transfers some of the momentum to the second billiard ball, which then moves away. The idea of a collision of objects is thus replaced with an idea of energy being transferred from one thing to another, but where even these things are just bundles of energy in a region of space.

What we have in causation is thus the transfer of a conserved quantity such as energy, momentum, or electrical charge. We can leave it to science to tell us exactly which quantities can be transferred between regions. When a rock hits a window, for instance, energy is transferred from it to the glass, which leads to it cracking. And when water is being heated in a kettle, energy passes from the electrical element into the water. Because conserved quantities are being passed from one place to another, such theories are often called physical transference theories or just transfer theories.

Understanding causation as a physical process could allow us to solve the well-known problem of common causes. Sometimes a cause has two distinct effects, which then look to be correlated and counterfactually dependent. When air pressure lowers, for instance, it causes both the barometer to fall and for it later to rain. This shouldn't be a problem but some theories of causation seem to make it so: they can make it look as if the falling barometer caused it to rain.

On the regularity view, for instance, it seems there could be a constant conjunction between the barometer falling and it raining, the barometer falls before it rains, and the rain occurs in the same place as the barometer. The case seems thus to satisfy the regularity definition of cause. Similarly, one might argue that rain counterfactually depends on the falling of the barometer: it doesn't rain unless the barometer falls.

We are pretty sure that this is a spurious case. The reason these two events are constantly conjoined is not because one causes the other but that they have a common cause: the drop in air pressure. And that is also the reason rain counterfactually depends on the barometer falling. But to claim there is a common cause, we must have some idea of cause in mind other than constant conjunction or counterfactual dependence (though this is not to deny that proponents of those theories think they can get around the problem in other ways). In a physical transfer theory, one could respond that there is a line of physical connection between the drop in pressure and the falling barometer, and one between the drop in pressure and rain, but none between the falling barometer and rain.

Reciprocity

Another purported advantage of such an energy transference account is that it accommodates and offers an explanation of the apparent asymmetry of causation. It will be recalled that Russell was suspicious of the philosophical notion of cause because it appealed to an asymmetry that he couldn't find in physics. Perhaps he needed to look harder. According to the transfer theory, effects gain energy, or whatever conserved quantity it is, and causes lose energy. There is thus a direction to causation: energy, momentum, charge, and so on, transfer from causes to effects.

This looks good for the theory but soon becomes a potential problem. Does the transfer theory always get the direction of causation right? Consider the case where ice cools a drink in a glass. When we say that ice cools we are using a causal term and we are attributing it to the ice. The ice is doing something to the drink. But the energy is not being transferred in that direction within this 'system' that is the glass, liquid, and ice. We shouldn't think of the ice as cooling the drink, therefore.

Various things could be said about this. There are a number of different transfer theorists and they disagree about some of the details. One thing that could be said is that it is merely apparent that the ice is doing something to the drink. What looks like causation in one direction is in fact causation in the opposite direction. The liquid is actually melting the ice, transferring its kinetic energy to it and in the process melting it. There is a true scientific explanation of this process and the popular understanding of it is just uninformed. It's a mistaken perspective that the ice cools the drink.

A more conciliatory note might be that it doesn't matter in which direction the energy flows. As long as there is a transfer of a conserved quantity between A and B, in either direction, then we have causation. Thus, whether energy is transferred from A to B, or B to A, there is causation going on.

The problem with such a concession is that the direction of causation—an apparent bonus of the transfer theory—is again lost. Perhaps that is not a huge price to pay, however. There is also a view, possibly inspired by Newton's third law of motion, that causation always involves reciprocity. Causation doesn't just change the effect: there is also an equal and opposite change to the cause. When the cue ball passes some of its momentum on to the object ball, it loses some of its own. Hence, while the object ball is caused to move by the cue ball, the cue ball is caused to slow down by the object ball. And the case of the ice in the drink shows this too. While the drink melts the ice, the ice cools the drink.

Rolling it out?

There may seem to be some plausibility in the cases discussed so far: balls colliding, windows smashing, and ice cubes melting. But this is supposed to be a theory about what causation is: all causation. Hence, this is to tell us what causation is not just in cases of small physical processes but generally. How plausible is this?

There are some large-scale processes that do seem amenable to the theory. The Sun warms the Earth, for instance, arguably by transferring energy across space to it. But what of some other cases that seem to be causal? In history, the killing of Archduke Ferdinand caused World War I. In economics, increasing the money supply causes higher inflation. In psychology, childhood experience shapes the adult. Can these diverse causal cases be put down to a transfer of energy, momentum, or whatever quantity?

The temptation is to say that these latter cases differ from those discussed earlier only in their degree of complexity. The sorts of events we discuss in history are likely to contain many, many smaller causal transactions as parts. And each of those could be a simple matter of energy being transferred around.

The sort of complexity that would be required would be huge, however. Do we have a good reason to believe it would all work out in the end? Much of causation in economics is not even about physically existing money being carried around. Many transactions are numbers being altered in accounts held on computers. And much else is about expectations of increased or decreased value or expectations of other people's expectations of increased or decreased value. The causal processes seem relatively easy to understand in terms of the explanatory mechanisms of economics but it seems inconceivable how one could cash that all out in terms of the passing round of quantities of energy.

Let us consider also the physical complexity of a psychological example. Within the explanatory concepts of psychology, the causation seems relatively easy to grasp. Traumas can be caused by someone breaking our trust, or from social exclusion. But how much would need to be in place for this to work out in terms of physical processes of energy transference? Just the simple concept of broken trust would involve so much physical complexity. There would have to be an account of a person's beliefs about another, beliefs that are historically situated within a perceived relationship and socially situated within shared norms of acceptable behaviour for interpersonal relationships. Can all this really be explained in terms of energy transference? What is passing energy to where, and what relevance does that have to causation? Does the energy transference really explain the causation?

Suppose that Tom likes Tina and Tina likes Tom. Tina accidentally touches Tom's knee and Tom blushes. There is some transference of energy here. Tina's hand passes on energy to Tom's knee when it presses it but how does that explain Tom's blushing? Ron could have pressed Tom's knee in exactly the same way, exerting exactly the same amount of energy on it, but Tom would not have blushed then. To explain the blushing we would have to include countless other factors: psychological, social, biological, and sexual. Could they all be explained in terms of energy transfer? There has to be at least some doubt that they can. And even if such an account were available in principle, it would probably be so unwieldy as to be completely incomprehensible to us.

Reducing to basics

An idea that might motivate a physical transference theorist about causation is reductionism. Indeed, such a commitment might be what would sustain a supporter of the theory in the face of the previous examples.

Reductionism is the view that all higher-level phenomena are explained in terms of lower-level phenomena, some of which are basic. Mechanistic philosophy would be one such example. One can observe a high-level phenomenon such as the turning of the hands on a cuckoo clock and then the mechanical bird appearing from a little door on each hour. We know, however, that if we look inside the mechanism we see smaller parts that are moving, and we can see how they are connected up and it is they that explain the turning of the hands and appearance of the bird.

Some of the parts within the clock may themselves have other smaller parts and the reductionist will think that any relatively high-level mechanism will have an explanation at a lower level. Eventually we come to a very lowest level in nature, however. Perhaps this is the level of subatomic particles. And while this lowest level can supposedly explain what occurs at higher levels, there is no lower level than this which explains the behaviour of its entities.

Now while many reductionists will be motivated by the scientific spirit, spurred on perhaps by some examples of apparently successful reduction in the sciences, reductionism remains a philosophical theory. It has no empirical proof. One might be impressed by the successes of biochemistry and think that therefore biology can be reduced to chemistry. But supposing even that this is a complete success, there are still other areas where we have not yet demonstrated how the reduction would work. And what argument, then, does reductionism rest upon? As things stand, fundamental physics cannot explain every higher-level case of causation.

Reductionists sometimes then state their view in terms of the finished or completed physics being able to explain everything else. But what is the basis for believing this, before all the evidence is in? Is it an inductive inference drawn from a handful of cases? That might not look very safe and it is hardly in the scientific spirit to prejudge on such empirical matters. Instead, perhaps we should think of reductionism as something like a working programme: something we are investigating to see how far we can go with it rather than asserting it to be a truth. That restores some modesty to the view.

There are some other difficult conceptual matters that the reductionist position has to face. One is that, for all we know, there might not be a bottom level in nature. As a matter of sheer philosophical principle, there is no reason why there has to be a very bottom level in the world, upon which everything rests. And just as we cannot know there to be a bottom level through our reasoning, nor is it the sort of thing that we could know from the evidence of the senses. The problem is that while we could know something is complex, by seeing that it has parts, we could never know that something is simple. It might after all have hidden parts that we have not yet detected. Some of the work done at CERN (the European Organization for Nuclear Research), for instance, attempts to establish whether some supposedly simple particles in reality have parts.

This particular issue might not be fatal to reductionism, however. The reductionist could maintain that higher-level phenomena are explained in terms of lower-level phenomena but deny that there is a very lowest level, or remain agnostic on it. But another issue cannot be avoided. Reductionism requires a stratified view of nature: that there are various levels to it, the relatively lower being more fundamental and explanatory than the higher. But what would these levels be? How are they defined and what are their boundaries? Is meteorology more fundamental or less so than economics? And are these facts about the world or more to do with our explanatory practices?

Emerging views

It needs to be made clear, though, that physicalism is not the same thing as reductionism. Some physicalists are attracted by reductionism but it is not inevitable that a physicalist hold that view.

There is also a view called emergentism, which allows that certain higher-level phenomena 'emerge' at that level and are not merely the sum of their lower-level parts. There may be something about emergent phenomena that thus will not allow, even in principle, an explanation at a lower level. There are some forms of emergentism that are anti-physicalist. Some are emergentists about the mind and mental phenomena, for instance. On this view, mind would be non-physical and non-physically explicable. But another form of emergentism would be simply that higher-level physical things are not mere sums of lower-level physical things and not explicable in terms of them. Instead, the higher-level phenomena could be indivisible wholes. Holism is a term that could be used for this view.

Why would someone think this? There are some cases where a higher-level entity really is nothing more than the addition of its parts, arranged in a certain way. The cuckoo clock is like this. But in other cases, when some of the parts come together to form a whole, they interact and change each other. Chemical composition sometimes exhibits this kind of change. When two elements come together to bond, doing so affects the chemical properties of the constituents so that the whole has a very different set of properties. Both sodium and chlorine are dangerous and harmful, for instance, but when they are chemically bonded in a certain proportion, they form sodium chloride: common salt. In certain proportions this is entirely harmless. Some of it is essential for human health, despite having lethal constituents.

If the properties of common salt are emergent from those of the constituents, having a very different set of causal powers from those of its parts, then how could we rule out that the causal powers in economics, psychology, biology, and sociology are emergent?

To repeat, however, this is not a challenge to physicalism as such. What it suggests is that there are certain higher-level phenomena that have to be treated holistically. They could be indivisible unities in the sense that to take them apart is to lose the causal role possessed by the whole. In that case, causation could occur at the level of the whole. Such an account coheres with the idea that economic causes have economic effects, biological causes have biological effects, and so on, and causal explanations should be domain specific. And if this is so, it might then be impossible to explain causation in these domains simply in terms of transference of energy or other conserved quantities at the micro level.

Empowerment

Considered as something that also occurs between wholes, causation becomes a bit more manageable. Human beings, for instance, are causal agents and patients. A man has the power to lift a rock, for example. We think of him as having free will. Might this be an emergent causal power, only to be attributed to persons—rather than, say, their neurons?

Opponents of free will point out that all physical processes are determined by prior causes. If causation is specific to a domain, perhaps this need not impinge on our free will. It is a man who lifts a rock; not even his arms and certainly not the molecules within his arms. And just as one can be a physicalist without being a reductionist, nor would the defeat of reductionism be the end of transfer theories. What is transferred could be something at a relatively macro level.

Chapter 7
Pluralism: is causation many different things?

We have seen three proposed theories of causation: that it consists in regularity, counterfactual dependence, or transfer of physical quantities. But we have also seen that there are counterexamples to each of these theories: where something meets the putative definition but does not look like causation or, vice versa, where something looks like causation but does not meet the putative definition. Does this mean that these theories offer the wrong definition of causation? Or could it be that any such non-circular definition will always be susceptible to counterexamples?

Each theory works well enough to pick out some and perhaps most cases of causation. Maybe there were a few exceptions but in general it seems clear enough that causation involves a degree of regularity, counterfactual dependence, or energy transference. The problem seems to be that for each theory there are one or two cases that don't fit the pattern. But should we infer from this that all the theories are wrong? Could it be instead that we are expecting too much of a single theory?

There is an assumption that causation is just one thing and that it is our business to discover its essence. Might we challenge this assumption? We sometimes use a single word to classify many different things. Consider the example of being a mammal. There are many different things that we call mammals: a whale, a human, a cow. The differences between a whale and a human are significant. A non-mammal fish resembles a whale more than does a mammalian human. Perhaps causation similarly permits a wide diversity of particular instances that have different features. This is what the pluralist says.

The reason all the theories we have considered have counterexamples, says the pluralist, is that they tried to pin causation down to one single thing, such as constant conjunction or whatever. Assuming none of these theories works alone, why not just take the disjunction of them? The form of a pluralist theory of causation is to say that where we have different theories *a*, *b*, *c*, and *d* that apply in some but not all cases, we should instead take causation to be their disjunction: causation is either *a* or *b* or *c* or *d*. If causation is a varied phenomenon, while some of its cases will involve constant conjunction, others will instead be cases of counterfactual dependence, energy transference, or whatever else is needed.

Causing in many guises

It has to be conceded that we seldom use the term 'cause' in everyday language. Contemporary pluralist Nancy Cartwright notes that there are myriad ways in which something can cause something else. We say that someone cut the tomato, kicked the ball, humiliated a friend, panicked the sheep, and so on. These are all specific cases of agency: things that humans can do or cause. And when we look at non-agent cases, we see the same. The nail punctured the tyre, a rock smashed a window, the wind blew the tree, the infection swelled the finger, and so on. We have various events or processes, therefore: cuttings, kickings, humiliatings, panickings, puncturings, smashings, blowings, and swellings.

These are the things that really go on in the world and causation is perhaps just a label we use to classify them all together. Maybe this classification is something only of interest to philosophers. Only a philosopher would say something like 'You caused the sheep to panic' instead of the more natural 'You panicked the sheep.' We seem to invoke a number of causal verbs in philosophical talk about causation: influence, produce, prevent, determine, control, interfere, counteract, enhance, increase, decrease, etc. Maybe there is nothing more to causation than the sum of these things.

And there are some who think the issue of causation is best left alone for the sake of scientific clarity. When a randomized controlled trial is conducted, for instance, the scientist is trained only to assert that there was a statistically better recovery rate with treatment T than without. Saying that T *causes* recovery is discouraged, perhaps because it is seen as making a metaphysical claim. At least, one might argue, it is clear what we are saying when we assert that statistically there is a better recovery rate with a treatment. What does it add to say that T causes recovery when there is actually no accepted theory of what causation is? That just muddies the waters.

Wittgenstein tackles Socrates

A philosopher's error, according to Ludwig Wittgenstein (1889–1951), is to assume that there must be a single essence to something just because we use one word for it. This error can be traced back to the philosophical methods of Socrates, one of the very first philosophers whose ideas have survived.

As catalogued in the writings of Plato, Socrates (*c.*469–399 BC) asked questions such as 'What is good?' 'What is justice?' 'What is love?' If he was presented with a specific example, such as justice being the paying of one's debts, he would insist that this wasn't the right kind of answer. That might be one example of justice but his interest was what justice was in general, in all cases.

Many philosophers have remained in the Socratic tradition of answering this kind of question. The philosophical theories of causation have been attempts to do this: to say that causation *is* constant conjunction, with temporal priority and contiguity, for instance. The claim is that this is what all cases of causation have in common and it is what makes all the particular instances causal.

A big challenge to this Socratic tradition came in Wittgenstein's later work, *Philosophical Investigations* (1953). Some of our notions, Wittgenstein said, could be thought of as family resemblance concepts. A family resemblance concept is one that groups together various different things on the basis of them having resemblances but where there isn't a single essence they all have in common.

If we consider a typical family, we tend to be able to tell that each particular family member belongs there. Perhaps three of the five family members have red curly hair but two of them don't. And maybe there is a family crooked nose but, again, not every one of the five has it. Again, there are brown eyes in most cases, but not all. Without there being a single 'essence' to this family—one single feature that they all share and makes each of them a member of the family—we are nevertheless able to recognize them as such. It might not even be possible for us to pin down exactly in what the resemblance consists, but we still think there is enough resemblance to enable us to recognize each of them as a member of this family.

Post-Wittgensteinian philosophers have wondered in various cases whether we are dealing with family resemblance concepts. It might naturally be wondered whether causation is a family resemblance concept, therefore. Stathis Psillos argues for this, following Elizabeth Anscombe. Some but not all cases of causation involve constant conjunction. Some but not all involve temporal priority, contiguity, energy transference, difference making, and so on. None of these features is either necessary or sufficient for

7. Family resemblance

causation. So there could be cases of causation where one or more may be lacking, and cases that are not causation but which exhibit one or more of these features. But cases that are causation will be ones that possess enough of these features such that we are able to recognize them as causal.

How many kinds of cause?

A recent pluralist view comes from Ned Hall. Just two concepts would do the job, according to Hall. Causation is either difference making or production. We are offered a simple disjunction of just two features.

In some cases, he says, what counts is that the cause produced the effect, even if it made no difference. We saw this in the case of an elk on the rail producing a train delay even though a signal was also stuck at red. Arguably the elk made no difference to the outcome but it did produce it. Similarly, when a firing squad of seven each fires into a hostage, we could say of each individual bullet that it produces the victim's death even though it makes no difference. Had one bullet not hit, six others did the job anyway.

But causal production is not enough, in Hall's view. There is some causation that works by making a difference even though there is no production. Suppose a doctor is about to administer a life-saving drug to a patient but the patient has an enemy. One way in which the enemy might cause the patient's death is by preventing the doctor from giving the drug. Prevention is difference making without production; indeed, it prevents a potential production.

Hall's pluralism suggests just two concepts of causation and something qualifies as causal by being either. But others have a more complicated picture. Hall's two concepts correspond roughly to what we have called physical transference and counterfactual dependence. We have seen that there is also the original Humean regularity view and there are other theories besides. Might it be then that the disjunction has more than just two disjuncts within it? Causation might be *a* or *b* or *c* or *d*. Or might the disjunction be completely open-ended? Perhaps there are some varieties of causation that we have not even encountered yet but would be included in our list if we did discover them.

And if we allow multiple kinds of cause within our long list, we then have some further questions to answer about what is enough to qualify as causation. Philosophers traditionally think that a disjunction is true if and only if at least one of its disjuncts is true. So *a* or *b* or *c* would be true if just *a* among them is true, for instance.

But we are not talking about pure logic here. Would we want to say, if there were many marks of causation, that satisfaction of just one of them was enough to qualify as a cause? We might instead say that there are various distinguishing features of causation and to qualify as a cause something must satisfy a good proportion of them but not necessarily all. Spatial contiguity might be a mark of causation, for instance. Not every case requires it, if there is immediate action at a distance; but also it would not be enough on its own to make something causal if it wasn't accompanied by some of the other marks of causation.

Aristotle's four causes

Aristotle (384–322 BC) spoke of there being four causes. We refer to them now as the material cause, formal cause, efficient cause, and final cause. Was he the first pluralist?

Any instance of causation will include all four causes, Aristotle thought. Two of these causes—matter and form—are intrinsic to any particular object. The material cause is the matter out of which something is made. This is what undergoes a change in the causal process. It could be the wood which is carved into a bowl, or the metal that is melted into the shape of a spoon. The formal cause concerns the form that the matter took, the bowl or the spoon, and is related to its function.

But the material and formal causes are not sufficient to cause the change. There has to be some extrinsic cause as well: the efficient cause that initiates the change. In the case of the bowl one needs someone to do the carving, and included in this is also the knife. For Aristotle there was also a final cause: the final aim or purpose of the change. The bowl was made for the purpose of serving soup, for instance.

There are different ways in which we could understand Aristotle's four causes. Some don't recognize them all as causes anymore. The concept of causation we mainly employ now develops the notion Aristotle called the efficient cause. But what are the others? Some think of them as explanatorily useful but not genuine causes, while others think of them as four conditions that are all necessary for causation to happen. Most contemporary philosophers of causation seem to think that the final cause is superfluous. It sometimes reappears in biology, however, such as when evolutionary success is thought of as the ultimate purpose of life.

Aristotle's four causes play different roles in the causal production of change. But is this the same as being a pluralist about causation? Could we say, for instance, that the efficient cause is a matter of energy transfer, while the material cause is a difference maker and the formal cause is a matter of regularity? Or is causation the same in each case: that there is something in virtue of which they all count as cases of causation, such as difference makers or necessary conditions? Perhaps they are a diverse bunch of phenomena that at most have a vague family resemblance.

Imposters

The problem with a family resemblance concept, whatever it concerns, is that resemblance on its own doesn't seem enough. A family could get an imposter: someone who looks a bit like the family members but who is not really one of them. Whales resemble most fish but without belonging to the fish family. Resemblance on its own does not seem to be enough to exclude imposters, therefore. What is needed is that the instances are resembling and members of the same family. But the latter issue just gets us back where we started, wondering what it is to be part of that family.

In the case of mammals, despite the diversity of the resembling 'family'—humans, whales, and cows—there is arguably a single thing that unites them. These diverse things are members of the mammal family because they give birth to live young and they suckle them. A fish resembles one particular mammal without being one because it does not have this feature.

Is there anything similar that we could say in the case of causation? It seems that we can distinguish correlations that are causal from those that are merely accidental. Accidental correlations would count as causal imposters. If there is something in virtue of which all the resembling cases are in fact instances of causation, rather than just looking like them, then perhaps this shows us what it is to be a cause. We would then have found an essence of causation: something that defines it.

But if there is no such thing that unites all the diverse cases, why do they really count as a united family at all? On what principle could one include or exclude imposters?

Making the right inferences

There is at least one attempt to explain what unites all the plurality of things we call causes without tacitly admitting there is a worldly essence to causation. What is common to all causal truths is that we use them to make a certain kind of inference.

If a match is struck, we can infer that it will light. If a window is hit by a rock, we can infer that it will break. And if an economy has received an increased money supply, we can infer that it will undergo further inflation. As with the standard pluralist position, these inferences are about various specific kinds of events but we assume that there is no worldly essence that they all share. There is thus nothing that they all have in common that we could call causation. But we call those things causal that we use in explanation and prediction of one natural phenomenon with another. Aristotle's four causes might then count as such.

This inferentialist position thus escapes one form of criticism against pluralism. The criticism could take the form of a dilemma. Either there is nothing that unites a resembling family, in virtue of which it is the causal family, or, if there is something that unites the family, then this looks very much like an essence of causation. The inferentialist view attempts to unite the family of causes not in virtue of them having a mind-independent, worldly essence, but in virtue of the epistemological facts of how we use them in our thinking.

But here there is an obvious issue. What makes something causal is not a fact about the world itself but something about our view on the world. Calling something causation just says something about how we think about it and what use we make of it to draw inferences.

So the inferentialist has avoided the dilemma faced by pluralism, but now faces another. Either such inferences really are about nothing more than our thoughts or they are about something happening in the world itself. If the former, then inferentialism is a form of anti-realism about causation. It just makes causation a feature of our thoughts: perhaps a figment of our imagination. If the latter, then isn't there something about the world that makes such inferences useful or broadly reliable? Don't we infer from one kind of fact to another precisely because that inference is often borne out? And isn't the most reasonable explanation of why such an inference is borne out simply that the two phenomena are causally related?

A concrete example might help. It is useful to draw an inference from the striking of a match to its lighting but it is not useful to infer from its striking to its evaporating. Why is this? A reasonable explanation would be that the first kind of inference is useful because striking matches causes them to light. The second kind of inference is useless because striking matches does not cause them to evaporate.

What this suggests is that causation should not be equated with the inferences themselves: causation would be that in the world which makes inferences reliable and useful. And might that thing be causation? Might it have a single defining feature or essence after all? In that case, pluralism might be thought of as just an admission of defeat. Are we giving up too easily on the attempt to find an adequate, all-encompassing theory of causation? There are still further options we can explore.

Chapter 8
Primitivism: is causation the most basic thing?

What if causation cannot be defined? Isn't it one of the most basic and fundamental things? In that case, perhaps other notions are defined in terms of it, but causation itself might be primitive.

We began by looking for accounts of causation that were effectively analyses. An analysis reduces one thing to another, thereby explaining it. The theories we looked at all seemed to leave an explanatory gap, however. There were some cases of causation that the theory could not capture; or the theory would rule something to be causation when it did not look to be so. Assuming that these theories all have shortcomings as analyses, there is more than one response we might have. One was outlined in the preceding chapter. We could say that causation was a plural concept where one theory applied in some case and a different theory applied in another.

There is a different kind of response, however. What about saying that any analysis would fail because causation is so fundamental that it is unanalysable? The whole project upon which we have embarked—of understanding causation in other terms—is thus one doomed to failure. The analytic strategy, so common in philosophy, would then be misguided in this case.

Analyse this

We saw how Wittgenstein challenged the idea that everything could be defined. An analysis is not quite the same as what we mean by a definition. It is more about what something is in the world rather than an explanation of the meanings of words. Philosophers tended to move from mere definitions to more worldly analyses and this remains a core project of the subject. We even had, in the early 20th century, the rise of so-called analytic philosophy.

If we take some troublesome philosophical notion, such as knowledge, the analytic programme was to break it down into its simple components. To *know* something—let's call it P, whatever that is—is a complex that consists in a number of other simpler facts. According to one classic account, to know that P, a person a must believe P to be true; P is indeed true, and a has a justification for believing P. We will not comment on the adequacy of this particular putative analysis. The point is to illustrate the method of analysis. Knowledge, on this theory, is accounted for entirely in other terms. Where this works, the analytic philosopher claims that they have reduced one thing to another: knowledge just is, nothing more nor less, than justified true belief.

For such a reduction to work, there cannot be any circularity. We cannot invoke in the analysis the thing that we are attempting to analyse. The analysis would then have failed. But it could fall short in another way too. There cannot be any part of the phenomenon that remains unaccounted for in the analysis. If the analysis works, whenever we speak of knowledge, we really are speaking about justified true belief.

Causation made simple

Although analytic philosophy might be considered a recent trend in the history of the subject, the basic approach can be found as far back as Locke. In his *Essay Concerning Human Understanding*, Locke tells us that many of our ideas are complex and built out of simple ones. The idea of a black cat is complex, for instance, containing simpler ideas of blackness, furriness, four-leggedness, and so on. The idea of blackness, however, could be absolutely simple. Using the simple ideas at our disposal, we can even construct complex ideas of things we have never seen. Having seen a cat, and also having seen the colour purple, we can form an idea of a purple cat even though no such thing exists.

If one adopts the Lockean framework, then, one might say that an idea such as knowledge is, despite any contrary appearance, a complex idea made up of the simpler ideas: for example, justification, belief, and truth. And if we want to understand how we could acquire the idea of knowledge, then we have to find the original experiences from which we gained these simpler ideas. An idea such as belief may itself also be complex and permit further analysis until we reach the level of absolute simplicity. This, it must be said, allows one possible criticism of the analytic approach: what if there are no absolutely simple things into which a phenomenon analyses? Could there be just more and more levels of complexity, all the way down?

Locke is seen as the founder of the British empiricist tradition of philosophy, where our ideas are seen as legitimate or not depending on whether they can be related back to original sense experiences. If we return to the question of causation, then the Lockean approach would be to wonder what the simpler components are from which we gain the idea of causation. Hume followed Locke's empiricist project and much of his work was on precisely this topic, as we have seen.

We could interpret the theories considered thus far as attempts to show what the more basic constituents are of causation. If we consider Hume's first theory again, we can interpret him as saying that causation is a complex phenomenon that is constituted by the simpler phenomena of constant conjunction, contiguity, and temporal priority, without remainder. But it is this final clause that his opponents dispute. They claim that there is something about causation that is left out of those three ingredients: you could have them all and still not have causation. The purported analysis fails, they might say, because there is something not captured by those three other, non-causal things. And the counterexamples to the theory reveal this.

And what if this is true of all purported analyses of causation? They might get close, but there is always some residue that cannot quite be captured in other terms. Perhaps there is a good reason for this. Causation might really be irreducible or primitive, which is what we mean by primitivism. There might be something unique about it. We could not, then, put something else in place of it and expect it to be exactly the same. Nor can we include anything causal in the analysis, on pain of circularity.

Going primitive

We wondered whether a move to pluralism about causation was just an admission of defeat. Various theories had been tried and failed, according to the pluralist, so by causation we couldn't mean just one thing: we had to mean a plurality of different things. Now again, no analysis works, says the primitivist, so let's just say that causation is unanalysable. Why isn't this just an admission of defeat? Isn't it a bit too easy to fall back on a primitivist response whenever we cannot find the right analysis? A lazy thinker might give up too soon and declare the impossibility of an analysis just because they cannot come up with one. What good grounds do we ever have, therefore, for going primitive about something? Is there a general principle that guides us?

One argument a primitivist might use in defence is that even within Locke's philosophy, and in analytic philosophy more widely, something has to be taken as basic. One has to be primitivist about something. Why shouldn't that thing be causation? As noted above, this part of the analytic approach could be challenged. If there is infinite complexity in the world, all the way down, then nothing would be basic after all. But we don't know for sure that this is true. And perhaps there is a level of nature that is as simple as we are capable of knowing. That might do for a relative primitivism about causation. It could be at least as simple as anything else we know, even if there is hidden complexity within it. The point is, however, that some primitivisms will probably be right, so there is nothing that is obviously wrong about making a primitivist move. It ought at least to be an option.

And perhaps it is a bit more than a merely possible option. There seems to be something going for it. We can think of causation as one of the most fundamental forces in reality: the cement of the universe. Causation is what holds objects together, through molecular bonds. It produces change in one thing by another. It gives an action significance. Why shouldn't this be one of the most basic elements of all? And then why would anyone ever think that we could account for causation in non-causal terms?

The whole of science seems premised on causation. That there are causal connections between distinct natural phenomena is the best interpretation we have of the regularity of the world, as evident to our senses or as revealed in statistical correlations. And if there is no causation responsible for producing the apparent degree of order in our world, then what else does? The relative orderliness of the world would be mysterious. And without that order—without those causal connections—science could not offer us predictions, explanations, or technology. So a core activity that has allowed human beings to flourish seems to be premised on the existence of causation. Why shouldn't we then be primitivists? Our whole engagement with the world is based on it.

Tables turned

The tables could be turned. Rather than analysing causation in terms of other, non-causal phenomena, don't we instead inevitably analyse other things in causal terms?

Vital in the empiricist philosophy is the thought that our ideas derive from our experience. Locke, for example, thinks that our ideas are formed by external objects that impress themselves upon our sense organs, such as sight. And Hume notes that an experience of regularity leads us to form an expectation about the future, which is at the root of his theory of causation. But in explaining this mechanism, which justifies the empiricist theory of experience, we have had to invoke causal connections at various places. External objects affect our sense faculties, for instance, and certain types of experience make us form an expectation. Impressing, affecting, making, and leading are, as we saw, specific causal terms.

The empiricist philosophy thus seems to depend on causation in order to work. So should it be in the business of reducing causation away into other things? Would the account still work once that reduction is offered? Hume is often criticized precisely on these grounds. The very approach that he uses to reduce causation away seems only workable if there are various causal connections in play, driving the habits of human thinking.

What is behind this line of attack is the plausibility of a causal theory of perception. Perception is important in the Lockean philosophy because it explains to us how ideas are legitimately acquired by the human mind. But what is it to perceive something? It seems that it is an irreducibly causal phenomenon. At the very least, to perceive F—whatever that might be—is for F to cause an idea or belief in the perceiver.

There might be a lot more to the analysis of perception than that. One might, for instance, say additionally that the idea or belief has to resemble or correspond to that which is perceived. But whatever supplementary claims were built into an analysis, one would think that a causal connection has to be in there somewhere. Our perception of the world is at the basis of everything we can possibly know. If the very possibility of any empirical knowledge rests upon there being causal connections between the world and our perception of it, then causation turns out to be the most fundamental thing of all.

Springboard to success

But there is yet another question in relation to perception. Is causation something that we can know about directly or is knowledge of it something that is inferred from perceptions of other things?

There is a very good reason to ask this question. Some ideas are primitive. But for them to be so, the empiricist requires that they be experienced directly. Such ideas have not been generated from other ideas, so the idea must have been acquired immediately. We needn't necessarily accept this view. Not everyone accepts this empiricist account of how we come to know things. But the primitivist will certainly protect their position against any empiricist attack if they can show that we do indeed have direct experiential knowledge of causes.

The Humean view is that we don't experience causation directly at all. When one billiard ball hits another, we cannot see a causal connection between them, only a succession of events. Causal knowledge for Hume was inferred from seeing repeated instances of such sequences: constant conjunctions. Not everyone agrees with Hume on this. A number of philosophers, going back at least to Thomas Reid (1710–96), think that causation is something that can be seen directly. But Hume's billiard balls are not the best place to look.

Consider instead when you watch a high diver jump from a springboard. The diver runs along the board, bounces and then dives into the water. When he jumps on the board, it bends under his weight and then he springs back up into the air. In such a case, even in a single instance, are we seeing causation? Are we seeing directly that the diver's jump, or his weight, causes the board to bend?

There are some philosophers who would say so. But the problem is that there is nothing in the case that would force a Humean to give up on their interpretation of what happened. The Humean could still say that if we saw such a case only once, we would not conclude that the diver caused the board to bend. Only through repetition would that idea come about.

Secret agent

A major factor has been overlooked, however. It has been staring us in the face, perhaps too close to see. Hume talked about causation as if we were outside observers. The philosopher might observe the game of billiards and the scientist might just record the correlations, neither of them interfering with what they see. Indeed, any experimenter has to make sure they don't influence the outcome. But, of course, they could.

We are not apart from the causal world. We are very much a part of it. We are causal agents: we initiate causation and our actions have effects. We are also causal patients: things are done causally to us. We are therefore both causally active and passive. Just like everything else, we have no escape from the causal web of the world.

It is almost as if Hume would keep this agency a secret. He says causation cannot be seen from watching the billiard balls collide but would he have said the same if he was in the position of the balls, doing the causing and having causing done to him?

Now given that we are able to cause things, might this be a place in which the causal primitivist could find some direct experience of causation? Arguably so. When you lift a heavy suitcase, for instance, you feel a strain in your muscles. You perhaps feel that it needs even more effort to succeed. The aching in your arm increases as you try harder but eventually the suitcase is lifted. You are the causal agent in relation to the lifting of the case and you feel the work being done, immediately in your body.

This sense, by which one feels one's force of effort, is known as proprioception. It is sometimes overlooked because it is not one of the classic five senses taught at school. But psychologists know that there are really more than just five senses and they think of proprioception as one of the additional ones.

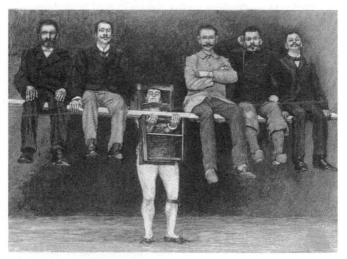

8. A causal experience

Proprioception gives us a sense of required effort. It is not just a matter of knowing when more effort is needed. We also use it to gauge when we are using too much effort. Suppose you go to lift the large case, for instance, that you don't realize is empty and is thus surprisingly light. The surprise realization forces you to readjust, lest you throw the case in the air. And it is not just in the case of action that we feel causation through proprioception. If someone pushes us, and in that respect we are passive, the resistance we exert to that action pressing upon us is also calibrated through proprioception. We resist the push so that we don't fall over backwards. But the resistance has to be proportional to the force experienced, so that we don't fall over forwards.

Humean beings?

Hume is aware that an opponent might try to claim that humans are causal agents that have direct experiential knowledge of causation. He tries to pre-empt this claim. His account of action is that we don't really experience that we are causing something. Again, he thinks our belief in our own agency comes down to nothing more than an expectation based on a constant conjunction of willing and moving. We will to do something and then our body moves in the appropriate way. A man wills to lift a case, for instance, and then his arm lifts it. And when this sort of thing happens many times, he starts to think of his willing as causing his bodily movement.

Do our actions really proceed in that way, though? Is the willing temporally prior to and distinct from the action itself? Hume has been criticized, by Wittgenstein among others, for separating the will and the act. While one can form hopes or intentions to act in the future, the act and the willing of the act seem to be simultaneous and inseparable. Suppose while lifting a heavy suitcase one suddenly lost completely the will to do so. Presumably one then stops lifting the case. And doesn't this show that the willing has to accompany the act at every stage to make the action operate? If the willing was temporally prior to the action, then how would it operate upon it? By the time the action has come, the willing has gone. And more than just accompanying the action, isn't the willing integral to it? It is constantly working upon the feedback gained proprioceptively to deliberately move in the required way for the achievement of the action's aim.

Much more could be said on this topic but some of the major issues have been outlined here. The case for primitivism about causation would be strengthened considerably if we were able to show that we have direct experience of it. Human actions seem the most likely place that we would get that. This does not mean that we are able to experience every case of causation directly. Much of our causal knowledge might well be inferred. But Hume was sceptical about how we could acquire any direct knowledge of causes at all. Just one case where we do so would answer that sceptical challenge.

Chapter 9
Dispositionalism: what tends to be?

To say of something that it has to be taken as primitive doesn't tell us anything substantial about it. In that respect, primitivism is not much of an informative theory. Suppose we agree that two different things are primitive: causation and something else. What, we could well wonder, is the difference between those two things, and between them and all the other things that are primitive?

It would help if we could say more about the nature of causation. The primitivist could still offer a theory of causation, where this falls short of reducing it away. They can say a number of substantial things about causation, differentiating it from other phenomena, even if it is not analysed.

A dispositionalist is someone who thinks that causation is essentially dispositional in nature. It is produced by causal powers being exercised, for instance. But those causal powers are not in a position to reduce causation away, for the notions of cause and power are too close. Power is already a causally laden term so not in a position to provide a non-circular analysis of causation. What is the dispositionalist theory of causation?

A powerful theory

In response to the regularity theory, there was a tempting thought that what happens at other times and places shouldn't be of relevance to a particular causal transaction. When water dissolves sugar, the Sun warms a room, a harm is caused, and so on, then the only particulars we need consider are those we have named. There can be a single instance of causation, this view maintains, irrespective of whether there is also a regularity. Indeed, regularities should only be thought of as sums of many single instances of causation taken together.

Dispositionalism trades on this singularist intuition. The view is built on the idea that individual objects can contain their own dispositional properties or, as some call them, causal powers. It is these that are responsible for any effects that those objects have.

A dispositional property is one that can exist unmanifested. When something is spherical, there is an idea that this feature is always available for our inspection, which is what we mean by manifested. But when something is fragile, soluble, or elastic, it suggests that there is some hidden potential within it. There is a disposition for some other possible property. That which is fragile has a potentiality to become broken, for instance.

But dispositionalists will often say that there are many other properties that are of this nature. If one takes spin, charge, and mass, for instance, some of the vital properties of subatomic particles, they can all be understood as dispositions to behave. A particle with a negative charge, for instance, has a disposition to attract other particles with a positive charge and to repel those that also have a negative charge. And charge is something that can come in degrees. There can be attractions and repulsions to greater or lesser degrees. The strength of a causal power can have a big say in what is eventually produced, which is a point often ignored when we think of causation as all or nothing.

There are some who think that all properties are essentially dispositional in nature. This view is called pandispositionalism. Even if one takes sphericity—the property of being spherical—one can see that things with that property will be disposed to behave in a certain way: to roll down a slope, for instance.

Pandispositionalism is not the only form of dispositionalism. One could think that some but not all properties are dispositional or causally powerful. But what marks someone out as a genuine dispositionalist is that they think dispositional properties are real and irreducible. And they are also properties that are productive of the behaviour of their bearers. Something's behaviour is explained as a manifestation of one of its dispositions. The connection with causation is apparent. Causal production is ultimately about the exercise of dispositions, which is why many call them causal powers, a term that draws attention to their causal role.

Dispositionalism is an ancient idea. Perhaps it is the very first theory of causation. It goes back at least to Aristotle and was continued through medieval times by St Thomas Aquinas (1225–74). It was against this well-established tradition that much empiricist philosophy was reacting. Hume gave us a completely new take on the question of causation, rejecting the causal powers view in favour of a regularity based theory of causation.

The empiricist dislike of powers has lasted as long as that tradition. We find it in J. S. Mill but also Russell, the logical positivists, and, through the spread of their influence, Americans such as Quine and Lewis. Such philosophers were sceptical as to the truly powerful nature of causation and treated it as something to be reduced away. Whenever they discussed powers it was so that they could offer a reductive account of them, turning them into properties that were occurrent or categorical, by which they meant non-dispositional. And since such properties would lack causal powers, they could not provide an ontological basis for causation, motivating the empiricist project of analysing causation in other terms.

More recent decades have seen a rise in neo-Aristotelian approaches to causation, however. This has often been motivated not by the great philosophers but by the idea that dispositionalism is the best way to make sense of causation in science or of contemporary metaphysical theories. The regularity and mechanistic views of the world are not the best explanation of what we know about causation, scientifically and metaphysically, according to these new views.

Getting technical

Dispositional properties seem essential for science as they provide explanation, prediction, and technical applications. We can explain the behaviour of some particular or kind of thing once we discover its dispositions to behave. We understand why two things stick together, for instance, once we understand their power of attraction. And if we understand that, we could start to predict possible behaviour in new situations.

If we take a large-scale engineering feat such as bridge building (Figure 9a), the structural engineer has to consider the causal powers of the main components: the girders, rivets, stilts, and suspension wires. They have to understand just how much weight each part is capable of holding: an as yet unmanifested dispositional property. Assuming the engineers get it right, then once all the parts are in place, they get to realize that potential.

One way a dispositionalist can explain technology is that it's all about unleashing and making use of hitherto hidden dispositional properties. When sticky black oil was first discovered, no one knew that it had within it so many different dispositions to behave. Would our ancestors have realized that it was able to burn, that it could be refined to make petrol that would fuel motor

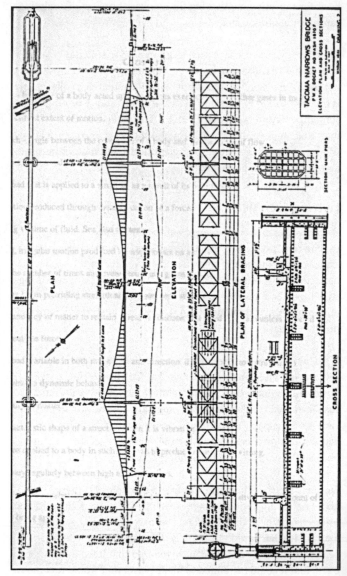

Causation

vehicles, and that it could be made into plastics? And might there still be unrealized potential within it? Or perhaps in some cleaner and more readily available source there is an ability to perform some of these same tasks.

Discovery in science is about finding the right condition to release causal powers. Who would have thought that the penicillin bacterium could have cured so many ills and who is to say there is not something simple and readily available that we could use to cure cancer or HIV, if only we knew how to use it? But the attempt goes on: a quest of discovery. Science advances through the discovery of new powers of things.

As Hume assumes

One common criticism of the regularity view was that we often think something stronger needs to be added to the regularity: a real causal connection that would rule out accidental correlations as genuine cases of causation. This might prompt the thought that causation must be constant conjunction plus some added ingredient.

But there is a line of thought that pulls in a different direction. It seems there are plenty of cases where we believe there is a causal connection even though there is not a constant conjunction. Almost everyone believes there is causation between smoking tobacco and cancer. There are lots of different things one could say about this but the feature to which we draw attention is that although we do not doubt that there is a causal connection, there is clearly no constant conjunction. Not everyone who smokes tobacco gets cancer.

If constant conjunction were considered a necessary condition for the establishment of a causal connection, then surely it would give us the wrong result in this case. We could call this the *fallacy of causal constancy*. It would be a clear mistake to think that because you know an old man who has smoked all his life without getting cancer, this showed that smoking does not cause cancer. What, then, does the causal claim amount to if it does not require an exceptionless regularity?

A necessary rethink

It was noted that necessity looks too strong for causation. It seems possible, and at the very least conceivable, that any cause may be thwarted by the addition of some extra factor. In our messy world, causal factors cut across each other, getting in the way of what could have happened otherwise. There are prevention and interference.

This was used in an argument to the effect that causes did not necessitate their effects. It was an argument that Hume himself used against causal powers. But now we see this argument doesn't automatically rule out causal powers. It would only do so if dispositions had to produce their effects by necessitating them. Now some have thought so, including Spinoza, whom Hume may have had in mind as his target. But it is arguable that both Aristotle and Aquinas thought differently: that a power only tended towards its manifestation.

The problem is that Hume presented us with a straight choice between absolute necessity and his own pure contingency view. It was relatively easy for him to show that necessity was implausible for natural causal processes. They could all be subject to interference. But the rejection of that view doesn't automatically prove that all is loose and separate, as Hume thinks, and that anything could in principle follow anything.

The third alternative, that Hume does not consider, is that causes tend or dispose towards their effects, where this is short of necessity but much more than pure contingency. We should not say that any possible outcome is just as likely. There is a definite tendency to one in particular.

With tendencies and their possible interferers, we can see how over a large population there need not be constant conjunction between causes and effects. Smoking can indeed be a cause of cancer where, for the dispositionalist, this means that it has a real causal power towards it. But this power is 'only' a tendency toward cancer, even though it is a pretty significant one.

What this seems to involve is that a number of those who smoke do indeed have the disposition towards cancer manifested. But there are others who benefit from the absence of factors that would have assisted the carcinogenic effect and presence of other factors that thwart the carcinogen. The development of cancer is known to be a very complex causal phenomenon and at each stage there is the possibility of prevention and interference. A lucky few may even have a genetic predisposition that works against cancer.

Another way of understanding this point is to think of dispositions as being highly context sensitive. One can vary the conditions of a power just slightly and it can have a big effect on how that power manifests itself, or whether it manifests at all. A good example of this is fragility. A fragile glass that is dropped might survive. But if one varies the circumstances just slightly, it could shatter into a hundred pieces. A small difference in the circumstances can produce a huge difference in outcome. Just one small additional factor could make the difference between whether someone gets cancer or not.

Nature and necessity

At this point, the dispositionalist might try to turn Hume on his head. He had insisted that regularity or constant conjunction were necessary for the idea of causation. One worry was that something more was needed. The dispositionalist could argue, however, that we don't need even constant conjunction. Indeed, a real, exceptionless constant conjunction might be taken as a good reason for saying that we do *not* have causation.

If we think of some good, well known constant conjunctions, do they turn out to be cases of cause and effect? All whales are mammals, for instance. But we have seen that this could be just a matter of classification. We have grouped whales within the class of mammals or, for an essentialist, nature has done the grouping for us. There is a regularity because it is a matter of necessity. Something could not be a whale without being a mammal. But doesn't this also show that it is not causation that is involved? Being a whale does not cause something to be a mammal. It is simply that the class of whales is a subset of the class of mammals.

Another case of constant conjunction also involves no causation at all. Some think that there are identities in nature, such as that between salt and NaCl or between Down's syndrome and having an extra chromosome 21. We certainly have constant conjunction here but we can guarantee it precisely because one thing is not causing the other. The constant conjunction occurs because we have just a single thing picked out with two different names.

The dispositionalist could then conclude that we should not expect pure regularity for natural causal processes at all. And wherever we find such constant conjunction, isn't that a good reason to doubt we have found causation?

Mutual manifestation

How, though, do powers produce their effects? We cannot take it for granted that they do so. Do they just spontaneously arise? It seems not. Effects are produced only when the conditions are right. Sugar is soluble, for instance, but to manifest that power it needs to be placed in water, which releases the power. Similarly, a fragile glass needs to be dropped or knocked before the power of fragility can do its work.

It is common to think that a disposition has to be stimulated. We usually speak of stimulus conditions, where the manifestation can be understood as the response. Coal is a flammable material, for instance, but it has to be lit in order to show it. Lighting could be thought of as the stimulus that allows the flammability to be revealed and then a process of burning to follow. For a long time it was thought that all dispositions were to be activated by their relevant stimulus conditions.

But some dispositionalists think that this is the wrong model of explanation. Charlie Martin preferred instead to think of dispositions forming mutual manifestation partnerships. They team up—sometimes in pairs but sometimes in bigger groups—to produce together what neither could have produced alone.

Instead of thinking of solubility as a disposition that gets stimulated by the addition of water, we should instead think of sugar and water as mutual manifestation partners for dissolving: for the production of a sweet solution. The problem with a stimulus–response model is that it suggests that dispositions are essentially passive: unable to do anything unless something else comes along and makes them act. This should not be an attractive idea to a dispositionalist, who tries to offer a more active view of nature. Here, the disposition is passive, and merely acted upon, while the stimulus is active. The stimulus then looks more powerful than the disposition itself, which is surely wrong-headed.

The mutual manifestation model makes groups of powers more or less equal partners in causation. They all add something and they all undergo change in doing so. The sugar is dissolved by the water, so suffers a change, but the water becomes a solute, holding the sugar in suspension. Similarly, the ice cube melts but it also cools the liquid. We can, therefore, have reciprocal changes in the mutual manifestation partners. Their coming together begins a natural causal process, which may take time to develop, and may be interrupted before it is completed, but is capable of producing change all round.

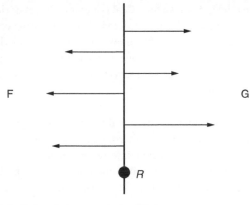

9b. Counterbalancing powers in equilibrium

But powers need not produce only change. Another possibility is of powers acting but producing no net change. Powers in opposite directions could result in equilibrium situations, like when vector addition produces a zero resultant R (Figure 9b). With the suspension bridge, for instance, we want all the powers to balance out so that the effect is stability: nothing happens. Some accounts of causation suggest that it is a relation between events, as we saw with Humean theories. But an important case is where the effect is that nothing happens, which would be a non-event. And in engineering we often do want to manufacture stability more than we want to manufacture change.

Are absences causes?

Dispositionalism tells us that causation is the exercise of a power or real disposition. Could that apply in every single case?

An alleged counterexample is causation by absence. Absence of water kills plants and absence of oxygen produces human suffocation. And one way to bring something about is by preventing it. A villain could see the death of his enemy by preventing someone from administering a life-saving drug. Could one account for cases like these in terms of the exercise of powers?

An option would be to say that nothingness could nevertheless be powerful. This looks hard to defend, however. Could the absent water have a power to kill your plant? That doesn't sound right. The absent water isn't anything at all, so how could it be causally powerful? There is one test of what it is to be real—the so-called Eleatic test—which tells us that to be real is to be causally powerful. If one took this line on absences being powerful, one would then be obliged to treat absences as part of reality.

But there is a different kind of approach. If the villain prevents the injection of a drug that would have saved his enemy's life, then the dispositionalist could say the following: What caused the death was the disease against which the drug would have offered protection. Now there might indeed be a true counterfactual that had the drug been received, it would have tended towards that person's survival (and this could be a counterfactual made true by the causal power of the drug). But that is not to give a cause of death. The cause was the disease. This still may be enough for the villain to have some moral or even legal responsibility for the death, if they stopped what could have prevented it. But such double prevention is not enough to make it causation, according to the dispositionalist.

Tending in the right direction

Dispositionalism can be viewed as a form of primitivism. Dispositionalists may try to uphold the idea that we can acquire the notion of causation through our bodily experiences as agents. And arguably we would also then get to experience the dispositional nature of that causation. An agent often feels resistance to their actions. They try to lift a washing machine, for example, but it is heavy. They can feel their action tending towards the lifting of it but also that the action can be prevented by the washing machine's weight.

But a dispositionalist is unlikely to offer this as an analysis of causation. Powers produce their manifestations. Production is already a causal term. So we cannot invoke the notion of a disposition to reduce away causation. The exercise of a disposition seems already to include it.

Dispositionalism does, nevertheless, offer us a theory: one that draws attention to certain features of the phenomenon. Causation can involve the action of singular objects in virtue of their real dispositional properties. It involves a tendency—but nothing stronger than a tendency—towards a certain type of outcome. This explains not only why causal production is not the same as necessity but also why causation is not about constant conjunction.

Dispositionalism can also be understood as a form of transfer theory, but without reductionism. Instead of saying that what is transferred is energy, causation will be the passing on of powers. A hot thing has the power to heat: when it does so it passes on that same power to the thing it heats. And the dispositional view also shows us why causes tend to make a difference. They often produce changes, though they need not always. But when they do, they will frequently produce changes that would not have happened otherwise.

Chapter 10
Finding causes: where are they?

The focus thus far has been with conceptual and ontological issues. This concerned what we mean when we say that one thing causes another and what causation is in the world. But there is a further question that is perhaps the crucial one for any science or technology. How do we find causes? Is there some method by which we can discover that one sort of thing is causally connected to another? How good is our causal knowledge? These are questions about the epistemology of causation.

It seems appropriate that these questions come last. We have to have an idea of what we mean by causation, and what we think it is, before we start looking for it. Those conceptual and metaphysical questions thus have to be first. But of course this also means that what one is looking for could be shaped by one's theory of causation. How a Humean searches for causes in the world could be different from how a pluralist looks, for instance, because these two have different views of what causation is.

Lies, damn lies, and statistics

It is sometimes said that you can prove anything using statistics. Sure enough, statistical methods have been adopted as a way of uncovering causal connections. That could work in some cases. One could note a statistical correlation, for instance, between children eating bananas for breakfast and improvements in their results at school.

The statistician's approach is to prefer lots of data. One child eating a banana and then getting a surprisingly good exam score would not be taken to mean much, if anything, from a statistical point of view. Suppose, however, we find that a whole group of children have eaten bananas on the morning of the exam and that, overall, the average score is significantly higher than when the children had other breakfasts. This may well be the discovery of a causal connection.

But how reliable is this method as a way of discovering causes? Arguably, not very reliable. The case may lead us to conclude that the bananas improved the children's performance but there could be other explanations that are consistent with the same statistical data. Another possibility is that having been told the bananas would improve their performance, the children approached the exam in a more positive frame of mind and this led to better results even though the bananas themselves did nothing. This would be a kind of placebo effect. Or there could have been other factors that made the difference: higher parental income, for instance. What this suggests is that if we do discover a causal connection from the raw data, then we would need a degree of luck.

Nevertheless, such an approach was seriously proposed by statistician Karl Pearson in his book *The Grammar of Science* (1911). The proposal was that we draw up what he called a contingency table that listed whenever one kind of thing was correlated with another. Pearson thought that such correlations should replace causal claims on the grounds of being more scientific. Instead of saying such things as A causes B, we should instead say that A is contingently accompanied by B (in such-and-such proportion of cases).

The obvious concern of such an approach is that it fails to distinguish genuinely causal correlations from those that are merely accidental. But if one has a traditional Humean view of the world, that distinction has less significance. All correlations are effectively accidental and contingent within the Humean framework. There never is more than the contingency table to go on. If A is regularly followed by B, then the Humean will ask what more we want in order to be able to say that A causes B. What does the causal claim add to the fact that A is correlated with B?

Statisticians often follow Pearson's idea that they have no business making causal claims. The job of statistics is just to report the facts: the data of what happens. Nevertheless, there is good reason to believe that even statisticians must have a view of causation as being something more than the data: something that generates the data perhaps. They have tried to develop more robust tools, precisely in order to eliminate the spurious correlations and find those that are more useful and informative.

The data alone, once we have large and detailed sets, show that basic correlations are problematic. One problem is that any statistical correlation can be cancelled out by the inclusion of other factors. Suppose, for instance, that the children to whom we offer bananas for breakfast also come from deprived backgrounds. Once we add poverty as an extra factor we might find that there is no improved exam performance. Or, as a more extreme case, suppose we add that the children have banana allergies. Clearly in that case it is unlikely that exam scores will be improved with their eating bananas. The scores may decline hugely. What one can show through statistics then seems largely to be dictated by what factors one assumes.

Ronald Fisher (1890–1962) had an idea of how to rule out the factors that could interfere with the data. We cannot know all factors that would have an effect, so we cannot pick them out one by one. But randomization can do the job for us. Fisher's idea is the basis of the randomized controlled trial (RCT), which builds on J. S. Mill's earlier *method of difference*. The RCT is to this day regarded by many as the perfect statistical tool for this job.

Recall that if we divide a large population into two groups randomly, then they should be more or less alike in all other factors that could interfere with a result. If we want to settle the issue of whether bananas improve exam performance we could conduct an RCT. We might have a group of 2,000 children and divide them randomly into two groups. There should then be just as many rich and poor children in both groups, just as many with banana allergies, just as many bright and not so bright children, and so on, if the randomization was done properly. The 'treatment' group gets bananas before their exams while the control group doesn't. If the results are better among the treatment group than the control group, then we declare that bananas improve exam performance.

Being particular

While the RCT remains the scientific gold standard, there are still some areas in which it is inadequate. The RCT measures for only one factor at a time and it has to do so over a large population. This can create difficulties. Because it is a measurement of a statistical trend over a number of interventions—those 1,000 children consuming bananas—then at best it could produce only a type-causal claim. The RCT tells us only about statistical averages. It is possible that some of the children in the treatment group have much better results after eating bananas but on others there is no effect at all. In some cases, like the allergy sufferers, the bananas could be detrimental to performance. The RCT still doesn't tell you whether one individual will do better in the exam if they first eat a banana. In deciding whether to eat the banana, therefore, a child might want to know whether they are typical for the group or not.

The other problem is that in testing for one factor at a time, the RCT cannot accommodate the point that causal factors may be highly context sensitive. Whether the banana works or not might be very sensitive to what else is present at the time of its consumption. We can sometimes have a cocktail effect where many different factors are brought together with an unpredictable outcome. It could be a limitation on the method, therefore, if one tests for each causal factor alone, one at a time, as if causal influences are discrete and isolated. In reality, they are probably not. But because the RCT deals only with statistical averages, the effects of context on the workings of a factor are likely to be hidden.

What matters to us is often the token causal truths—the truths of what particular causal connections there are—rather than generalities. If a drug has been on average shown to increase health, it could nevertheless be very important to one individual that on them it has the opposite effect and perhaps could even kill them. Are there then any ways of searching for causes in the particular case?

Mapping complexity

A highly influential contemporary account comes from Judea Pearl. Pearl's idea is that we understand causation on the model of a causal graph (Figure 10). The graph can represent complex causal set-ups in which there are numerous connections between the different elements. The graph is based on the simple idea that if one performs a 'surgical' intervention to change the cause, it can result in a change in the effect. A window might be closed, for instance, but opening it makes it more probable that the room will cool down if there is a causal connection between the window being open and room temperature dropping.

There are many other factors that could affect room temperature. Perhaps if one opens the window while also turning on a heater, the room will not cool down after all. The surgical operation is designed just to vary one factor, while leaving the others as far as possible unchanged. Of course, it might be that there are some things that would change also along with the opening of the window. Perhaps its opening makes it more likely that someone will turn on the heater, to stop the room getting cold. What we need, therefore, is a complex model that shows a number of factors to be involved, with numerous connections between those factors.

The causal graph shows the connections where intervening on one factor or variable would raise the chance of another factor occurring or variable being raised. The graph shows not just what happens but also what would happen if something else occurred. To understand all these possible connections is to have what Pearl calls a deep understanding of the situation. It is the sort of understanding an engineer would have when they look at a circuit diagram. They would be able to see what output would be

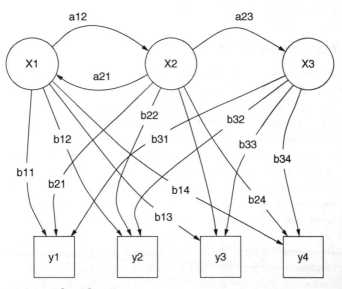

10. A causal graph

generated in response to a certain input. If a certain switch were to be turned on, for instance, what would also follow from it?

Getting your hands dirty

We should note here a major new idea. It is one thing to sit back and record the statistics concerning what follows what, but if we want to discover causal connections one obvious thing is to intervene: make a change and see what happens with it. Science could be completely passive and merely catalogue the facts, or it could be active, making changes as part of an investigation. This idea has been developed by James Woodward.

Even before we get to the rigour of science, intervention does seem an intuitive way of discovering causal connections. We are active in the world all the time, lifting, pulling, pushing, pressing, sometimes using tools to assist us. One turns the tap and finds that water comes out; and then turns it back and finds that it stops. One heats food and finds that it cooks. One kicks a ball and finds that it moves, but finds that the same operation performed on a big tree does no such thing. As causal agents and patients, we are constantly interacting with the world, pushing and probing to see what that makes happen.

Suppose that we were presented with a black box, the inner workings of which are hidden to us, but on the outside of which are various levers, pedals, and buttons as well as lights, bells, and buzzers. How are we to find what causes what? The answer is that we intervene: pull a lever and see if anything else happens. Does a light come on? And does it go off as soon as the lever is returned to its starting position? Does the same light still come on if a pedal is also pushed at the same time the lever is pulled?

There are all sorts of 'experiments' we can perform on the black box. We might not get immediate and certain causal knowledge of the connections between the various components, but our interventions at least enable us to start forming hypotheses. The experimental method is founded on this basic idea. Sometimes to find causes, you have to get your hands dirty.

There is another very simple idea that forms a basis for the interventionist account of causation. In abstract terms, you can change the effect by changing the cause. So if there is a causal connection between rising temperatures and people wearing fewer clothes, you can raise the temperature in a room and make it more likely that the occupants will undress. But you cannot raise the room temperature merely by undressing.

There is of course a limitation on the experimental method. There are some factors that we are incapable of controlling but which nevertheless can be causes. The Sun warms the Earth, for example, and those of us standing on its surface. This is as clear a case of causation as any. And yet we are entirely incapable of intervening to raise the temperature of the Sun, lower it, or turn it off completely.

Interventionist approaches tend, therefore, to take a broad notion of intervention that does not mean the narrow range of changes that we humans are able to affect. Why, after all, should our notion of cause be so anthropocentric? An intervention can mean, therefore, any change in a cause, whether it has been done deliberately by us or not. Thus, if it starts to rain, it will make people hold umbrellas. This is an 'intervention' on the weather, one outside our control. And given that people holding umbrellas does not make it rain, it is clear that the asymmetry is back into causation.

Take a chance

In Pearl's causal graphs, the arrows connecting the factors (or 'nodes') depict probabilistic connections, which Pearl understands in Bayesian terms, which is why they are sometimes called

Bayesian networks. Bayesianism is one particular account of how we should understand and adjust our probability assessments in the light of new evidence. The idea that a cause is something that raises the chance of its effect is attractive but controversial. Setting that discussion aside, it can still be said that there are two very different ideas of what probabilities consist in.

There is a view known as frequentism, which states that the facts about probability are fixed by the relative frequency of occurrence. Thus, a frequentist is tempted to say that the fact that the coin has a 50:50 chance of landing heads is that in the history of events, roughly half of tossed coins have landed heads. For those who think so, a statistical approach is obviously helpful.

There are also propensity theorists, however. They think that even in a single case, there can be a determinate propensity towards an occurrence, with a particular strength. One could say, then, that a coin has a 50 per cent propensity towards landing heads no matter how many times it is actually tossed, and indeed whether it is ever tossed at all. Statistical facts about frequencies of occurrence will be determined by the inherent propensities of objects, rather than vice versa.

Take control

The issue of large-scale frequency data versus singular propensities could inform one's approach to finding causes in the world. Someone who is tempted by the singularist approach might wonder what the point is of repeating an experiment many times over. Perhaps one well controlled experiment, where all the interfering factors are carefully screened off, would be enough to find a causal connection.

Suppose one was working in the early days of chemistry and wanted to discover what, if anything, happens when one chemical element is added to another. In nature, most things come in mixtures and one might never have had a chance to observe a true case where the pure elements are mixed. The chemist then seeks out the pure elements and keeps them carefully stored in test tubes, avoiding outside contaminants. A measured quantity of one can be added to a measured quantity of another and we can then observe what occurs.

If this experiment has been properly controlled, haven't we already done enough to establish the causal connection? A singularist could well think so, though Humeans may have doubts. The same experiment might have been run countless times over as time passes, in school chemistry classes, for instance. But schoolmasters are not asking the pupils to contribute to the proof of the result. The effect of mixing the chemicals is already established and an unexpected result would almost certainly be blamed on experimenter's failure from the pupil. Once the causal connection has been revealed in a single, reliable case, the repetition of the same experiment adds nothing further. As in school, the repeating of the experiment is mainly for training purposes. It is not as if teachers are Humeans looking to add to the stock of constant conjunctions.

Nancy Cartwright supports this kind of experimental method as a way of finding causes but she also raises a problem with it. Once one has found a cause this way, what is the external validity of the experiment? How can one use such causal knowledge when in the 'real' world, outside the laboratory, such causal factors are subject to all the usual interference and preventions of our messy world? The experiment tries to isolate a causal factor in something like a closed system. But in all the other cases we know, the world acts as an open system, with unexpected factors coming in from all directions with all sorts of consequences.

A symptomatic approach

Having considered various experimental methods for the discovery of causes, we ought to acknowledge that causation can be discovered in different ways, some more reliable than others. To give an indication of the signs of causation, we could consider the old Bradford Hill criteria of causation, proposed by Sir Austin Bradford Hill in 1965. The suggestion was that to find causation (in epidemiology, in this case), one should look for nine factors: for example, the strength of association, its consistency, its temporal priority, the strength of a dose being proportional to strength of response, and so on.

One might think these criteria insufficiently general to apply to causation in all domains, and one might reject some of them. But the idea of looking for the things that are reliable symptoms of causation seems sound. As we have suggested, however, what those symptoms are will depend on what one takes causation to be: one's philosophical view.

Some have taken the constancy of the relationship to be a prerequisite for causation. A dispositionalist would tend to disagree with this. Absolute regularity could suggest it is not causal at all and to understand causation is in part to understand it by way of failure: that effects can be prevented from occurring. One could nevertheless then look for signs of general tendencies, difference making, stability under intervention, and so on. This is not to resort to a form of pluralism. Even if causation is a single thing but primitive, we might still be able to find it via its symptoms.

A very short afterword

Causal knowledge is crucial in understanding, prediction, and our ability to form new technologies. Yet again, it is indispensable in every science and social science. We cannot ignore causation and still function in our world. Philosophers and scientists working together offer the best hope of a rounded understanding of this most vital of connections in the whole universe. With that understanding, we will know which symptoms best lead us to the causes. We have offered some hints in this book. As most scientists, statisticians, and philosophers will acknowledge, however, such symptoms are only a guide—a fallible one—to where the true causes lie.

Further reading

General

Anscombe, G. E. M. (1971) *Causality and Determinism*, Cambridge: Cambridge University Press.

Beebee, H., Hitchcock, C. and Menzies, P. (2009) *The Oxford Handbook of Causation*, Oxford: Oxford University Press.

Russell, B. (1913) 'On the Notion of Cause', in Mumford, S. (ed.) (2003) *Russell on Metaphysics*, London: Routledge.

Sosa, E. and Tooley, M. (1993) *Causation*, Oxford: Oxford University Press.

Humeanism

Hume, D. (1748) *An Enquiry Concerning Human Understanding*, P. Millican (ed.), Oxford: Oxford University Press, 2007.

Mackie, J. L. (1980) *The Cement of the Universe: A Study of Causation*, New York: Oxford University Press.

Psillos, S. (2002) *Causation and Explanation*, Chesham: Acumen.

Counterfactual dependence

Collins, J., Hall, N. and Paul, L. A. (2004) *Causation and Counterfactuals*, Cambridge, MA: MIT Press.

Physical transference

Dowe, P. (2000) *Physical Causation*, Cambridge: Cambridge University Press.

Kistler, M. (2006) *Causation and Laws of Nature*, New York: Routledge.

Pluralism

Cartwright, N. (2007) *Hunting Causes and Using Them*, Cambridge: Cambridge University Press.

Hall, N. (2004) 'Two Concepts of Causation', in Collins, J., Hall, N. and Paul, L. A. (2004) *Causation and Counterfactuals*, Cambridge, MA: MIT Press.

Psillos, S. (2010) 'Causal Pluralism', in Vanderbeeken, R. and D'Hooghe, B. (eds), *Worldviews, Science and Us*, Singapore: World Scientific Publishing.

Dispositionalism

Ellis, B. (2001) *Scientific Essentialism*, Cambridge: Cambridge University Press.

Harré, R. and Madden, E. H. (1975) *Causal Powers: A Theory of Natural Necessity*, Oxford: Blackwell.

Martin, C. B. (2008) *The Mind in Nature*, Oxford: Oxford University Press.

Mumford, S. and Anjum, R. L. (2011) *Getting Causes from Powers*, Oxford: Oxford University Press.

Interventionism

Woodward, J. (2003) *Making Things Happen: A Theory of Causal Explanation*, Oxford: Oxford University Press.

Causation and law

Hart, H. L. A. and Honoré, T. (1959) *Causation in the Law*, Oxford: Oxford University Press, 2nd edition, 1985.

Moore, M. S. (2009) *Causation and Responsibility*, Oxford: Oxford University Press.

Causation and science

Illari, P., Russo, F. and Williamson, J. (2011) *Causality in the Sciences*, Oxford: Oxford University Press.

Causation and social science

Elder-Vass, D. (2010) *The Causal Power of Social Structures: Emergence, Structure and Agency*, New York: Cambridge University Press.

Hoover, K. D. (2001) *Causality in Macroeconomics*, New York: Cambridge University Press.

Causation in medicine

Howick, J. (2011) *The Philosophy of Evidence-Based Medicine*, Oxford: Wiley-Blackwell.

Finding causes

Pearl, J. (2009) *Causality*, 2nd edition, Cambridge: Cambridge University Press.

Causation and probability

Mellor, D. H. (1971) *The Matter of Chance*, Cambridge: Cambridge University Press.

Suárez, M. (2011) *Probabilities, Causes and Propensities in Physics*, Dordrecht: Springer.

Further reading

Index

Index

SOCIAL MEDIA
Very Short Introduction

Join our community

www.oup.com/vsi

- Join us online at the official Very Short Introductions **Facebook** page.
- Access the thoughts and musings of our authors with our online **blog**.
- Sign up for our monthly **e-newsletter** to receive information on all new titles publishing that month.
- Browse the full range of Very Short Introductions online.
- Read **extracts** from the Introductions for free.
- Visit our library of **Reading Guides**. These guides, written by our expert authors will help you to question again, why you think what you think.
- If you are a teacher or lecturer you can order inspection copies quickly and simply via our website.

Visit the Very Short Introductions website to access all this and more for free.
www.oup.com/vsi

INTERNATIONAL RELATIONS
A Very Short Introduction
Paul Wilkinson

Of undoubtable relevance today, in a post-9-11 world of growing political tension and unease, this *Very Short Introduction* covers the topics essential to an understanding of modern international relations. Paul Wilkinson explains the theories and the practice that underlies the subject, and investigates issues ranging from foreign policy, arms control, and terrorism, to the environment and world poverty. He examines the role of organizations such as the United Nations and the European Union, as well as the influence of ethnic and religious movements and terrorist groups which also play a role in shaping the way states and governments interact. This up-to-date book is required reading for those seeking a new perspective to help untangle and decipher international events.

www.oup.com/vsi